THE HISTORY OF ETHIOPIA

A. H. M. Jones

Elizabeth Monroe

Simon Publications
2001

Copyright © 1935 by Oxford University Press.

First published in 1935 by Clarendon Press, Oxford

Original title: The History of Abyssinia

Library of Congress Card Number: 36001712

ISBN: 1-931541-62-0

Printed by Lightning Source Inc., La Vergne, TN

Published by Simon Publications, P.O. Box 321, Safety Harbor, FL 34695

PREFACE

THE object of this book is to present to the general public an accurate and comprehensive account of the history of Abyssinia within a moderate compass. The book is divided into six parts. Part I deals with the origins of Abyssinia, mythical and historical, its evangelization, and its contacts with the Roman Empire. Part II covers the dark age when Abyssinia was cut off from the rest of Christendom by the rise of Islam. Part III describes the discovery of 'the kingdom of Prester John' by the Portuguese early in the sixteenth century, and the attempt of the Jesuits to convert the country to the Catholic faith. Part IV covers the second period of isolation which followed the expulsion of the Jesuits down to the collapse of the monarchy at the end of the eighteenth century. These four parts are contributed by Mr. A. H. M. Jones. In Part V Miss Elizabeth Monroe describes the resurrection of the kingdom in the nineteenth century and its relations with the European powers which occupied the neighbouring lands and endeavoured to establish themselves in Abyssinia itself. The dispute with Italy, which, whatever its outcome, clearly marks the opening of a new chapter in Abyssinian history, is separately treated by Miss Monroe in Part VI.

In a work of this scale much has perforce been omitted, and a certain dogmatism on obscure points, especially in the story of the origins, has been inevitable. Similar qualifications must be made for what is written of recent events where very often the full facts are not obtainable. Finally, in the spelling of proper names simplicity has been preferred to pedantic accuracy. Diacritical marks have been omitted. When European equivalents of personal names exist they have been used (e.g. Claudius for Galadewos).

CONTENTS

PART I

i. THE COUNTRY 1
ii. THE PEOPLE 7
iii. THE LEGENDARY ORIGIN OF THE KINGDOM . 10
iv. THE HISTORICAL ORIGIN OF THE KINGDOM . 21
v. THE CONVERSION OF THE KINGDOM . . 26
vi. THE CIVILIZATION OF THE PRIMITIVE KINGDOM 31
vii. THE ABYSSINIAN CHURCH . . . 35

PART II

i. THE DARK AGE OF ABYSSINIA . . . 44
ii. THE RESTORED SOLOMONIAN LINE . . 53

PART III

i. PRESTER JOHN 59
ii. THE MEDIEVAL CIVILIZATION OF ABYSSINIA 63
iii. THE PORTUGUESE EMBASSY . . . 76
iv. THE MOSLEM INVASIONS AND THE PORTUGUESE EXPEDITION 81
v. THE JESUIT MISSION—OVIEDO . . . 88
vi. THE JESUIT MISSION—PAEZ . . . 92
vii. THE JESUIT MISSION—MENDEZ . . . 96
viii. ABYSSINIA IN THE SEVENTEENTH CENTURY . 101

PART IV

i. THE PERIOD OF ISOLATION . . . 108
ii. THE COLLAPSE OF THE MONARCHY . . 120

CONTENTS

PART V

i. 1770–1870. THE STRUGGLE AMONG THE GREAT CHIEFS 127
ii. 1870–1916. THE EMPERORS VERSUS THE POWERS 134
iii. 1916–1934. THE GROWTH OF A MODERN STATE 159

PART VI

1934–1935. THE DISPUTE WITH ITALY . . 175

INDEX 185

LIST OF ILLUSTRATIONS

THE OBELISKS OF AXUM	*facing p.* 34
THE CHURCH OF THE REDEEMER OF THE WORLD AT LALIBALA	50
PAINTING FROM A MS. OF KING YEKUNO AMLAK, FOUNDER OF THE RESTORED SOLOMONIAN LINE . . .	50
PRESTER JOHN'S KINGDOM, FROM ORTELIUS (1570) . .	78
THE NORTHERN MOUNTAINS OF ABYSSINIA. AN AIR PHOTOGRAPH	134
MAP	*at end*

PART I
i. THE COUNTRY

BETWEEN the valley of the Upper Nile and the plains of Somaliland rises a vast block of mountains, the homeland of the Abyssinian people. The eastern edge of this irregular plateau is clearly defined. Its rim is formed by a range of mountains, which, rising some hundred miles south of Suakim, runs for two hundred miles along the Red Sea coast to Massaua and then turns due south for four hundred miles till it reaches the neighbourhood of Addis Ababa. This mountain wall, which scarcely projects above the general level of the plateau on its western side, drops abruptly on the east from a height of some seven or eight thousand feet to the sea and to the plain of Danakil. South of Addis Ababa the edge of the highlands is not so clearly marked. The main range turns southward, stretching to Lake Rudolf. It no longer, however, is the boundary of the highlands. Over against it rises another block of mountains, the Arussi country, and from this block another range, the mountains of Harar, stretches eastwards towards the Gulf of Aden. These mountains slope gradually down into the plains of Somaliland, of which they form the northern frontier. The main block of the Abyssinian highlands, enclosed on the east by a crescent of mountains, whose northern tip adjoins the Red Sea and whose southern tip touches Lake Rudolf, tilts towards the west. On the west it is bounded by no definite range. It descends irregularly in vast terraces to the valley of the Nile.

Owing to its great altitude the Abyssinian plateau enjoys, despite its nearness to the Equator, a comparatively temperate climate. It is cool by contrast with the torrid plains of Danakil and Somaliland, which bound it on the east and south-east, and the deserts of Nubia and the steaming basin of the Upper Nile which bound it on the north-west and west. For the same reason it attracts a heavy rainfall, which is almost entirely concentrated in the summer months. In this also it contrasts with most of its neighbours. Only in the Upper Nile basin is there a comparable rainfall. The Danakil and Somali country is so arid as to be mainly desert. Nubia is utterly desert save where it is watered by rivers. The general tilt of the Abyssinian plateau being towards the west, its drainage is for the most part in that direction. Only one river flows east, the Hawash, which, rising near Addis Ababa, makes its way towards the Gulf of Aden but fails to reach it, losing itself in lagoons in the sandy plains west of Jibuti. Only one river flows south from the main block of the Abyssinian highlands, the Omo, which also fails to reach the sea, feeding the land-locked Lake Rudolf. Two other rivers flow southwards from the Arussi country. Neither is considerable and only one of them, the Juba, reaches the sea; the other, the Webbe Shibeli, is swallowed by sand-dunes near the coast. By far the greater part of the rainfall of Abyssinia drains north-west to the Nile. Three great tributaries feed the Nile from the Abyssinian mountains: in the north the Takazzé, known in its lower course as the Atbara, in the south the Sobat, and between them the Abai. The Abai flows from a huge lake, sunk deep in a depression in the heart of the mountains, Lake Tsana. It turns first south-east and then describing an enormous loop emerges in a north-westerly direction from the mountains as the Blue Nile. The tremendous gorge which the river has cut for itself through the mountains is one of the most impressive features of the Abyssinian landscape, and, presenting as it does an almost insuperable barrier to communications between Gojjam and the southern highlands, has played an important part in Abyssinian history.

It is the swelling of the Abai by the summer rains on the Abyssinian mountains which causes the annual rise of the Nile in Egypt. On Abyssinia thus depends the life of Egypt, a fact of which both the Egyptians and the Abyssinians have long been well aware. Many fantastic legends of the Middle Ages bear witness to the belief that the Abyssinians held the life of Egypt in their hands. In the history of the patriarchs of Alexandria it is written that in A.D. 1093 the Nile failed to rise, and the Caliph, suspecting the true cause, sent the patriarch laden with rich gifts to the king of Abyssinia. The king yielded to the prayers of his spiritual overlord, and in one night the Nile rose three cubits. According to Abyssinian legend one of the later kings of the Zagué dynasty, who reigned in the middle of the thirteenth century, formed the grandiose scheme of drying up the infidel land of Egypt altogether, and began to deflect the rivers of Abyssinia to the Indian Ocean. When he had diverted three or four, the scheme was abandoned, either because the king died, or, according to another account, because the priests represented to him that in destroying Egypt he would make of the arid plains of the infidel Somali a rich and fertile country, and thus raise up another Moslem power at the very gates of Abyssinia. In 1325 King 'Amda Seyon stayed a persecution of the Copts by threatening their oppressor, the Sultan el Nasir, that he would make Egypt a desert. Even in the early sixteenth century the great Albuquerque, viceroy of the Indies, entertained the same idea. One of his grandiose schemes for destroying the Venetian monopoly of the Indian trade and diverting it to the Cape route controlled by the Portuguese was to persuade the king of Abyssinia to make Egypt an impassable desert by cutting off the Nile. In recent years the king of Abyssinia has approved a more modest scheme for damming the Abai where it emerges from Lake Tsana, but the object of this scheme is not to desiccate Egypt, but so to regulate the flow of the river that less water may run to waste to the sea in the flood season and that Egypt and the Sudan may thus enjoy a more copious and regular water supply.

By contrast with the surrounding plains the Abyssinian highlands may be termed a plateau; their general level is some six or seven thousand feet above the plains. They are, however, far from being a plateau in the sense of a level elevated plain. Above the general level of the plateau rise many irregular mountain ranges, some as high above it as it is above the plains. In the centre of the highlands sinks a deep depression, whose bottom is filled by Lake Tsana; the surface of Lake Tsana is three thousand feet below the level of the plateau. The plateau is, moreover, intersected by the channels which the many rivers have cut for themselves. Many of the rivers flow some thousands of feet below the general level of the highlands, sometimes in wide valleys, often in precipitous gorges which form impenetrable barriers to communication. The whole aspect of the country is indeed wild and fantastic in the extreme. Its strangest and most characteristic feature is the shape assumed by many of its mountains. These often take the form of truncated cones, flat on top with almost sheer sides. These ambas, as they are styled, form almost impregnable fortresses, for the few paths which scale their precipitous flanks can be held by a handful of men against an army and on the wide plateau on top ample crops can be grown and herds of cattle can pasture, so that the garrison need never starve. The ambas have played a great part in Abyssinian history. They have been the last strongholds of unsubdued native tribes and of rebels who defied the Abyssinian kings; they have been the refuge of the Abyssinians when their country was overrun by foreign invaders. Many of them are occupied by monasteries, which have thus enjoyed some security in the many invasions and civil wars which have ravaged the country. They have served as treasure houses for the kings and as prisons for political offenders of high degree. One played a strange role. On it were segregated all the males of the royal house save the king and his sons: cut off from all communication with the outside world they could not distract the kingdom with rebellions, and on their lonely plateau they lived and died save when one was summoned to the throne when the direct royal line failed. In a country so well endowed with natural fortresses and so divided by lofty mountain ranges and deep river gorges unity is hard to achieve. The kings have always found it difficult to maintain their hold on the several provinces, each of which is cut off from its neighbours by natural barriers of great strength. Rebellion and civil war have always been frequent. Untamed tribes have been able to maintain their independence for long periods. At times the kingdom has broken apart into a number of virtually independent principalities. It is a wonder that Abyssinia has been able to achieve the substantial unity which it has enjoyed almost throughout its history, and a great tribute to the strong national sentiment and dynastic loyalty of the Abyssinian people.

In their impenetrable mountain home the Abyssinian people have always lived a life apart. Their one channel of communication with the centre of Mediterranean civilization has been their harbours on the Red Sea coast; for the land route to Egypt across the Nubian desert has never been of importance. Through these harbours they have exported the natural products of their own and neighbouring lands, gold and ivory, pepper and spices, incense from the plains of Somaliland, negro slaves from the Upper Nile, and in more modern times coffee, whose original home is the province of Kaffa in the southern highlands. Through these harbours they have imported the products of industry from the Mediterranean world, and with them the seeds of civilization. By this route came the first invaders from southern Arabia who brought with them the national language and script of Abyssinia. Greek culture filtered in by this route, carrying with it Christianity, the national religion of Abyssinia. By the same route the first Western visitors, the Portuguese, introduced the elements of modern Western civilization. But this single line of communication has never been secure and has often been broken. For long periods, especially since the rise of Islam, the Abyssinians have lived cut off from the outside world, and during those periods, in which they were surrounded by barbarians and enemies of their faith, they developed a distrust of foreigners. This distrust was unhappily fortified by the conduct of the first of their co-religionists of the West with whom they came into contact, and for many centuries after communications with Europe had been reopened the Abyssinians deliberately shut their doors to foreigners. For the greater part of their history the Abyssinians have thus lived isolated from the outside world, fostering the delicate plant of their faith and culture, defending it against the onslaughts of foreign foes, and developing it unaided and uninstructed. Little wonder that it has grown into a strange and fantastic tree.

ii. THE PEOPLE

The primitive inhabitants of the Abyssinian highlands would seem to have been peoples of Hamitic stock, racially and linguistically akin to the Danakil and Somali peoples to the east and south-east and to the tribes of the Nubian deserts to the north-west. In the south-western part of the highlands these Hamitic peoples have been strongly modified by the infiltration of negro tribes from the Upper Nile, and both in language and racial type they differ markedly from the peoples of the central and northern plateau. In prehistoric times—the date is quite uncertain, but probably falls in the first half of the first millennium B.C.—Arab tribes from Yemen crossed the Red Sea and landing on the African coast gradually occupied the northern part of the highlands. Of these tribes one, the Habashat, has given to the country the name, Habesh, by which it is still known to the Arabic-speaking world and from which is derived the European name of the country, Abyssinia—more correctly, as in German, Abessinien. Another, the Agʿazi, has given its name to the classical language of the country, Geʿez, in which all its ancient literature is written and which is still the liturgical language of its Church. These Arab tribes, gradually conquering the indigenous Hamitic population, intermarrying with them and imposing upon them their language and culture, formed the nucleus of the Abyssinian people, which is thus predominantly Semitic in culture, but predominantly Hamitic in blood; to the Arabs of Arabia the Abyssinians have always, despite their Semitic tongue, been the Blacks. These semitized Hamitic peoples were gradually consolidated into a kingdom, the Kingdom of Axum, which covered roughly the province of Tigré. The kingdom first came to light in the first century A.D. In the fourth century it was converted to Christianity. Cut off from the sea in the seventh century by the rise of Islam, it turned its energies southwards, and during the dark centuries which followed it gradually conquered, converted, and absorbed the aboriginal peoples of the central highlands. By the thirteenth century the provinces of Amhara, Gojjam, and Shoa had been almost completely assimilated. Only in a few inaccessible regions remnants of the Agaus, as the Abyssinians style the primitive inhabitants, preserved their Hamitic speech and pagan religion. For the rest the people adopted the Christian religion and the Semitic speech of the conqueror. The proportion of Semitic blood which filtered into the newly conquered regions was naturally very much smaller than in the original kingdom. The language also underwent modifications as it became diffused, and the Amharic dialect, which is generally spoken in the central highlands and is now the official language of the country, is farther removed from the classical Ge'ez than is the dialect of Tigré. The subsequent conquests of the Abyssinian kings in the southern highlands have not had so deep and lasting an effect on the native population. Many districts, even so far south as Kaffa, have adopted Christianity, but they retain their original Hamitic tongues.

From the fourteenth century the Somali peoples, who had been converted to Islam, began to invade the highlands. They continued to do so for several centuries, but with little permanent result. The object of their invasion was plunder and destruction and they made no settlements. Early in the sixteenth century began a movement which was profoundly to modify the Abyssinian kingdom, the immigration of the Gallas. The Gallas are racially closely allied to the Somalis. Their original home is uncertain, but is probably to be sought in the outlying highland mass which lies between the Abyssinian plateau proper and the Somali plain. From the sixteenth century onwards they have flowed in successive waves into the main plateau of Abyssinia and have occupied great parts of the southern highlands, leaving the aboriginal population scattered in enclaves cut off from one another and from the semitized population of the central highlands; it is in large measure due to the Galla invasions that the aboriginal population of the south has not been assimilated like that of the central highlands. Some Galla tribes have even penetrated into the central highlands; the Wollo Gallas, for instance, have planted themselves between Shoa and Amhara. The Gallas were pagans when they invaded the country and for the most part remain so in practice. Some tribes, like the Wollo, have become fanatical Moslems. Others have received a faint tincture of Christianity, honouring Jesus and Mary among their gods.

The centre of gravity of the Abyssinian kingdom has steadily moved southwards. The capital, originally at Axum in Tigré, has moved gradually to places farther south. For a while it was in Gondar, in Amhara north of Lake Tsana. At the end of last century it was fixed at Addis Ababa in Shoa. The Abyssinian kings gradually lost control of northern Tigré. Massaua was occupied by the Moslems, and the Nubian Beja tribes overran the coastal districts. At the present day the northern half of Tigré is included in the Italian colony of Eritrea; its population is, however, still to a large extent Abyssinian in language and in religion. The core of the Abyssinian kingdom has been from the Middle Ages and still is the central highlands, Amhara, Gojjam, Shoa, and southern Tigré. These districts are substantially Christian and Amharic speaking, though enclaves of the primitive Agau peoples still preserve their ancient Hamitic tongue in remote districts and intrusive Galla tribes have established themselves here and there. The modern kingdom includes many districts to the south and east over which the old kings never ruled or at best exercised a very shadowy suzerainty. It includes the southern highlands, which are inhabited by a hotchpotch of Hamitic peoples and Galla tribes. In this direction the kings of the fourteenth to the seventeenth century had from time to time exercised effective sway and had introduced Christianity, but the modern kingdom stretches farther than their most distant conquests, incorporating some pagan negro peoples in the extreme south-west. The modern kingdom also includes the outlying south-eastern highlands, the home of the Galla people, and a vast but sparsely populated tract of inner Somaliland. These conquests date only from the latter part of last century.

iii. THE LEGENDARY ORIGIN OF THE KINGDOM

The kings of Ethiopia—for the Abyssinians reject the name which the European and Arabic world gives to them and prefer to call themselves Ethiopians—trace the origin of their line to King Solomon. The most generally accepted version of the story runs thus: When Solomon was building the temple he sent messages to all the merchants of the four quarters of the world to bring him what he required and he would pay them in gold and silver. Among the merchants who responded to the call was Tamrin, the merchant of Makeda, the Queen of Ethiopia, who brought red gold and sapphires and black wood that could not be eaten by worms. He was struck with amazement at the splendour of Solomon's kingdom and the wisdom of Solomon himself and brought back such a marvellous report of him to the queen that she determined to visit him herself. So she set forth with a great caravan of seven hundred and ninety-seven camels and mules and asses innumerable laden with gifts, and arriving at Jerusalem presented herself to the king. Solomon entertained her honourably, giving her food in abundance and eleven changes of raiment every day. She stayed many months marvelling at the wisdom with which Solomon directed the artificers and communing with him on matters of religion, and before long she abandoned the worship of the sun and the moon and the stars and worshipped the God of Israel. At length, after six months she resolved that she must return and look to her kingdom. When Solomon heard of her purpose he said in his heart, 'A woman of such splendid beauty has come to me from the ends of the earth. Will God give me seed in her?' The chronicler is here at some pains to justify the polygamous habits of Solomon, which, he explains, were not due to lust but to the desire to raise up many sons who would inherit the cities of the heathen and destroy their idols. So Solomon determined to fulfil his purpose, and he invited the queen to a great farewell feast, and served dishes full of pepper and vinegar such as would make her thirst. At the conclusion of the feast, since it had drawn late, he invited the queen to sleep in his palace. The queen hesitated, but at length consented if Solomon would swear not to take her by force, for she was a virgin. The king agreed, and demanded from her in return an oath that she would not take by force anything that was in his palace. To this she agreed without demur, protesting that she was not a thief. So two beds were spread on either side of the royal bedchamber, and they retired. The queen slept a little, but presently she awoke and her throat was parched. Now the king had bidden his servants set a jar of water in the centre of the room. The queen espied it and was filled with longing, and when she thought that Solomon was asleep she crept out of her bed and put her hand to the jar. But Solomon had not been asleep, and he leapt out and seized her arm and said: 'Thou hast broken the oath that thou hast sworn not to take anything by force that is in my palace.' The queen protested that the oath did not apply to water, but the king replied that there was nothing upon earth more precious than water. The queen admitted that she was wrong, but begged that she might drink. So Solomon was released from his oath and he worked his will on her, and they slept together. And as he slept the king dreamed a dream, and he saw that the sun came down to the land of Judah and illumined it very brightly, and presently it removed to Ethiopia and shone there. And a second time it came to the land of Judah, but the Jews hated it and strove to destroy it, and it departed to the lands of Rome and Ethiopia.

Next day Solomon gave to the queen a ring, saying: 'If thou hast a son, give it to him and send him to me.' And the queen departed to Ethiopia and she bore a son, and she called his name Menelik. And when he had come to man's estate he wished to go to his father. And the queen gave him the ring, and sent him forth with a great retinue under the charge of Tamrin the merchant, and she bade Tamrin ask King Solomon to anoint Menelik king and make a law that from henceforth none but the male issue of Menelik should rule in Ethiopia—for hitherto queens had reigned in Ethiopia. And so Menelik travelled to the land of Judah, and when he came to Gaza the people made obeisance to him and cried, 'Hail, the king liveth.' And others said, 'The king is in Jerusalem, building the temple.' And they were perplexed and sent messengers to Jerusalem and there they found King Solomon and they said to him: 'Behold, one has come to our land who resembleth thee in every feature.' And Solomon asked whence the stranger came and they said, 'We asked him not, for he seemed to be one of great authority, but his followers said that they were of Ethiopia.' And King Solomon rejoiced in his heart, for, though he had married many wives, God had confounded his purposes and he had but one son, Rehoboam, a boy of seven years. And he summoned Menelik to Jerusalem and Menelik gave to him the ring, but Solomon said, 'What need is there of the ring? Without a sign I know thee that thou art my son.'

Then the merchant Tamrin delivered the message that the queen had given to him. And Solomon tried to persuade Menelik to stay and reign in Israel, for he was his first-born son. But Menelik would not. And so King Solomon anointed Menelik with the holy oil of kingship, and named his name David, and made a law that henceforth only his male issue should reign in Ethiopia. And Zadok the high priest expounded to him the law of Israel and pronounced upon him blessings if he should keep it and curses if he should leave it. And Menelik, for so his mother had commanded him, begged of Solomon a piece of the fringe of the covering of the Ark of the Covenant, that the Ethiopians might reverence it, and Solomon promised to grant his desire. And moreover Solomon summoned his counsellors and officers and said to them: 'I am sending my first-born son to rule in Ethiopia. Do ye also send your first-born sons to be his counsellors and officers.' And they obeyed the king's command.

And when the time came to set forth, the sons of the nobles of Israel were sorrowful at leaving their native land and secretly reviled Solomon. Here the chronicler inserts an excursus on the wickedness of reviling kings and murmuring against them. But their greatest sorrow was that they must leave Our Lady of Zion, that is, the Ark of the Covenant. And Azariah, son of Zadok the high priest, thought of a design, and binding the others to silence he revealed it to them, and they rejoiced greatly. And they each gave to him ten didrachms of silver, and he went to a carpenter and said to him: 'Build me a raft; for we are to journey across the sea, and, if the ship sink, so shall I be saved.' And he gave to the carpenter the measurements of the Ark of the Covenant. And the night before they were to depart, he took the raft, which was of the form of the Ark, and went to the temple and entered into the sanctuary—for the angel of the Lord opened the doors for him—and he took the Ark and put in its place the raft and covered it with the three coverings of the Ark so that none could see the change.

And the next day Solomon bade Zadok take the outer covering of the Ark and bring it to him. And Solomon gave it to Menelik and Menelik rejoiced in the gift. And Menelik and the first-born sons of the nobles of Israel set forth in a great train of wagons. And the wagons were lifted up about a cubit from the earth and they sped quickly like eagles and in one day they went thirteen days' journey. And when they came to the land of Egypt the sons of the nobles of Israel revealed to Menelik how they had brought the Ark with them, and Menelik was filled with joy and skipped like a young ram before the Ark. And they went on their journey and came to Ethiopia. And Menelik ruled in Ethiopia and his sons after him and the sons of the nobles of Israel and their sons after them were the counsellors and officers of the kingdom.

And when Menelik had departed Solomon was sad at

LEGENDARY ORIGIN

heart, and he told Zadok of the dream that he had dreamed the night that he lay with the Queen of Ethiopia. And Zadok was smitten with fear and said: 'Would that you had told me of this dream before, for I fear that Our Lady of Zion is departed.' And he went into the sanctuary and took off the two under coverings and beheld the raft of planks which Azariah his son had caused to be made. And he wept and beat his breast and fell in a swoon. And presently another came and saw and brought word to Solomon. And Solomon arose with his host and marched to Egypt and he questioned the Egyptians when the Ethiopians had passed. And they answered that they had passed many days before. And Solomon despaired of pursuing them and lamented greatly. But the spirit of prophecy comforted him saying: 'Our Lady of Zion has not been given to an alien but to thine own first-born son.' And Solomon was comforted and returned to Jerusalem. And he charged all his counsellors and officers to keep secret the loss of the Ark of the Covenant, and so the children of Israel knew not that it had departed.

Now Balthazar, king of Rome, had no son but only three daughters. And he sent to King Solomon and asked that he would send one of his sons to marry one of his daughters and rule over the kingdom of Rome. And Solomon sent Adramis, his youngest son, and with him the youngest sons of his counsellors and officers. And Rehoboam ruled over Judah, and Menelik ruled over all the lands to the south and to the east, and Adramis ruled over all the lands to the north and to the west. And so was fulfilled the prophecy that kings of the seed of David and Solomon should rule over all the world. And there was another prophecy that the king of Rome and the king of Ethiopia should rule the whole world, their kingdoms meeting in Jerusalem. And this was fulfilled in the latter days, for the Jews lost their birthright, slaying the Son of God, and Justin, king of Rome, and Kaleb, king of Ethiopia, destroyed their kingdom.[1] And after that the kings of Rome also lost their birthright, being led astray by Arius and Nestorius and abandoning the true faith, which is the faith of Alexandria. And so the kings of Ethiopia, the descendants of the first-born son of Solomon, alone are the heirs of the promises.

The legend is, it need hardly be said, entirely apocryphal. It is a sufficient refutation of it that the kings of Axum down to the fourth century A.D. were pagans and boast on their monuments their descent from Mahrem, a god of war. Its motives are fairly plain. Three principal motives operated in forming the legend. The first was the desire of the Abyssinian people to prove their ancient origin. Parvenu peoples, like parvenu individuals, hanker after ancestors, and peoples have as little scruple in forging family trees as have individuals. The Romans, when they came into contact with the older civilization of Greece, became painfully aware of their recent origin, and, searching among the epic legends describing the fall of Troy and the wanderings of the heroes, grafted on to them the story of the Trojan hero Aeneas, who migrated to Italy and whose descendants founded Rome. Similarly the Abyssinians, coming into contact with the civilization of the Christian East, desired to find a place for themselves in its ancient history. The only historical literature which the Abyssinians possessed was the scriptures, and so they searched the scriptures for allusions to themselves. Their earlier efforts were rather unhappy. They knew that the Greeks called their country Ethiopia. In the scriptures they found that Ethiops was the son of Ham—for in the Septuagint Cush is rendered Ethiops. They therefore

[1] This alludes to an historical event. *Vide inf.*, p. 30.

proudly adopted the name of Ethiopians, the name by which they call themselves to this day, thus affiliating themselves to Noah. Their choice of an ancestor was not altogether fortunate, for although there are a few complimentary references to Ethiopia in the scriptures, such as 'Ethiopia shall soon stretch out her hands unto God', there is no doubt that Ethiops with all the descendants of Ham fall under the curse of Noah, that they shall be slaves. An affiliation to the more honourable house of Shem was clearly desirable.

At this point the second motive comes into play. God had given great promises to Abraham and Isaac and Jacob. The Jews had forfeited their birthright by rejecting the Messiah. In a spiritual sense no doubt the Christian Church was the heir to the promises, for all Christians were spiritually of the seed of Abraham. But this spiritual interpretation has failed to satisfy many simple minds, who crave for a literal fulfilment of the promises in favour of the blood descendants of Abraham, and, observing that their own nation is obviously the chosen people, by a very natural inference deduce that it must be descended from Abraham. The desire to inherit the promises has produced in modern times among persons who should know better many fantastic legends, according to which the Saxons are the sons of Isaac and the British Empire the promised kingdom. The Abyssinians may therefore be pardoned if they, moved by the same desire, concocted a legend which is at any rate more plausible than the theories of the British Israelites. The obvious starting-point of the legend was that mysterious Queen of Sheba who came from the ends of the earth to hear the wisdom of Solomon and of whom our Lord had said, 'The Queen of the South shall rise up in judgement with the men of this generation and shall condemn them.' Her enigmatic figure had gathered round itself a tangle of fantastic legends, many of which are reproduced in the Koran. Her dominions had already in the first century A.D. been located by Josephus in Egypt and Ethiopia.[1] It was only necessary to give her a son by Solomon to link the blood royal of Ethiopia with the house of David. The kingdom of Ethiopia was thus affiliated to the kingdom of Israel, and to assure the seniority of the Ethiopian kingdom Menelik was made the first-born son of Solomon and the Ethiopian nobility were made the first-born sons of the nobles of Israel, and finally the Ark, the visible sign of God's presence among his chosen people, was transferred to Axum. But the Abyssinians were not churlishly exclusive. They recognized that all Christian kings had an equal right to inherit the promises, and they therefore traced back the lineage of the only other Christian king of whom they knew, the Roman emperor, to Solomon, but to a younger son.

The third motive that may be detected in the formation of the legend is the desire of the royal house of Abyssinia to assert their divine right to the throne. By tracing their descent to Solomon, by making him anoint the first king of their line with the holy oil of kingship, and by attributing to him the Salic law of Ethiopia, the kings of Abyssinia invested themselves with an aura of divinity. Revolt against them was sacrilege, for were they not the cousins of Christ?

The date at which the legend was formed cannot be fixed with any precision. What may be called the authorized version of the legend, the *Kebra Nagast*, or Glory of Kings, was composed at the beginning of the fourteenth century, and was evidently intended to justify and glorify

[1] In the Septuagint Sheba is spelt identically with Seba, the son of Cush (Ethiops). This is probably the reason why Sheba was placed in Africa and not, where it really was, in Arabia.

LEGENDARY ORIGIN

a new dynasty which had ascended the throne in about A.D. 1270 and which claimed to be a restoration of the Solomonian line. The legend was, however, not, as might have been suspected, invented for the benefit of this dynasty. A colophon to the *Kebra Nagast* states that it is a translation from an Arabic version made in A.D. 1225 from a Coptic original in the patriarchal library of Alexandria. This is not very good evidence, but it is fortunately confirmed by an impartial outside authority. Abu Salih, who wrote a history of the churches and monasteries of Egypt at the beginning of the thirteenth century, knew of the legend. He records that the Abyssinians possess the Ark of the Covenant, in which lie the two tables of the Law, written by the hand of God. He adds that the kings of Abyssinia are not of the house of David but are descended from Moses. These words imply that the legitimate royal house was that of David, and the dynasty which reigned in Abu Salih's own day, the Zagué kings who were ejected in 1270, were intruders. It is suggestive that these kings claimed a pre-Solomonic descent—their connexion with Moses, of which nothing else is recorded, was presumably based on Numbers xii. 1, where it is stated that Moses took a Cushite (in the Septuagint Ethiopian) wife. It suggests that they had found it necessary to raise a counter-claim against the dynasty which they ejected, and that that dynasty, which fell in about 1150, already claimed Solomonic descent. The legend can thus be traced to the beginning of the second millennium A.D. It is probably not so early as the sixth century A.D., for the Greek writers of that date know nothing of it but state that the Abyssinians are a colony of Syrians transplanted to Ethiopia by Alexander the Great.[1] It was, then, probably in the dark

---

[1] A highly obscure and abbreviated Greek inscription on the coins of one of the early Abyssinian kings (fourth to sixth century) has been

centuries that followed the rise of Islam, when the Abyssinians were cut off from all contact with the rest of the Christian world, that the legend arose. It had already taken firm root by the middle of the eleventh century and rendered the position of the usurping Zagué kings precarious. During the dominion of the Zagué kings it was reduced to literary form at Alexandria, the patriarchs of which seem, as the spiritual heads of the Abyssinian kingdom, to have opposed the intruding dynasty at first. This literary version was finally translated into Ge'ez under the auspices of the new dynasty which overthrew the Zagué kings and claimed, whether truly or not cannot be said, to be a restoration of the old Solomonian line. Thereafter the legend was canonical. In the early sixteenth century, when first we have an account of Abyssinia by a European, it was firmly believed that the Ark of the Covenant reposed in the cathedral of Axum, that the royal line was descended from Solomon, that the hereditary officers of the royal court were Israelites, and that the hereditary order of priests who served the royal churches were of the line of Zadok. Belief in the legend has continued to flourish down to modern times. The royal copy of the *Kebra Nagast* came to be regarded with superstitious reverence and when it was carried off to England by Napier in 1868, John IV, the successor of Theodore, found that his subjects would not recognize his authority. He wrote in 1872 to Lord Granville: 'There is a book called *Kebra Nagast* which contains the law of the whole of Ethiopia and the names of the princes and churches and provinces are in the book. I pray you will find out who has this book and send it to me, for in my country my people will not obey my orders without it.' The

read 'King of Habesh, King of Sion', but the interpretation is so doubtful that it cannot be treated as evidence.

Trustees of the British Museum were moved by this pathetic request and restored the book to the king.

The legend of the Queen of the South has had an importance in Abyssinian history quite out of proportion to its historical value. The consciousness that they were the chosen people, the guardians of the Ark of the Covenant, and the heirs to the promises made to Abraham, has done as much as their pride in upholding the orthodox faith of Alexandria to maintain the courage of the Abyssinians in their perpetual wars against their Moslem and pagan enemies. Their belief that their royal house is descended from the royal house of Judah has given a remarkable stability and continuity to the kingdom and has maintained the unity of a country which is from its geographical structure difficult to hold together. The dynasty which established itself in A.D. 1270 reigned with scarcely a break till 1855.[1] During the last century of its existence, it is true, it reigned but did not rule, but few kingdoms can boast a dynasty that reigned for nearly six hundred years and ruled effectively for nearly five hundred. There have been rebellions and civil wars in plenty in Abyssinian history, but the ideal unity of the kingdom under its divinely appointed dynasty has always remained in the background, to re-emerge when a strong king of the line of Solomon arose to reassert his prerogatives.

iv. THE HISTORICAL ORIGIN OF THE KINGDOM

The first European visitors to Abyssinia were the Greek admirals sent out in the third century B.C. by Ptolemy II and III of Egypt to explore the western coast of the Red

[1] The present dynasty claims Solomonian descent, but only through the female line.

Sea. The object of these expeditions was partly to open up trade with the interior, but more particularly to capture African elephants which the Ptolemaic kings trained for military purposes and pitted against the Indian elephants of their rivals the Seleucids. The Ptolemies established a number of trading and hunting stations along the coast, one of which, Berenice the All Golden, probably occupied the site of Adulis, the future port of the kingdom of Axum. As the Ptolemaic power declined, these stations were gradually abandoned, but the commercial relations which had been formed were kept up.

The Abyssinian kingdom is first mentioned in the *Periplus of the Erythraean Sea*, a description of the coasts of the Red Sea and the Indian Ocean written in the latter half of the first century A.D. The author describes the port of Adulis and states that eight days' journey inland lay the metropolis of the Axumites, whither was carried all the ivory from beyond the Nile and whence it was exported to Adulis and so to the Roman Empire. The king of all these regions, he adds, is Zoscales, 'a covetous and grasping man but otherwise noble and imbued with Greek education'. Zoscales must then rank as the first historical king of Abyssinia, and in his day civilization was already following in the footsteps of commerce.

Our next item of information comes from a curious source, the *Christian Cosmography* of Cosmas. Cosmas was a merchant, probably of Alexandria, who sailed the Red Sea and the Indian Ocean in the early sixth century A.D. In his declining years he retired into a monastery and devoted the remainder of his days to writing a book to refute the impious pagan theory that the world was spherical in shape and prove that it was in fact a flat oblong, twice as long from east to west as it was broad from north to south. To prove his thesis Cosmas draws principally upon the

HISTORICAL ORIGIN

Scriptures and upon the works of pagan men of learning, whom he delights to refute out of their own mouth. But occasionally he justifies his argument from his personal experiences. In one of these personal anecdotes he relates that while he was on a visit to Adulis the king of Axum sent orders to the governor of Adulis to copy two ancient Greek inscriptions in the town. The governor requested the learned merchant to do this for him, and Cosmas took two copies, one of which was dispatched to the king and the other was published subsequently in the *Christian Cosmography*. One of the inscriptions dates from the period when Adulis was a Ptolemaic station and records the exploits of Ptolemy III. In the other an Abyssinian king recounts his numerous warlike expeditions. Most of these were directed against peoples of Tigré, but some penetrated farther afield. The king subdued the mountainous country of Semien, south of the Takazzé (which he calls the Nile). He conquered the peoples of the vast waterless plains whence came incense and perfumes (Danakil). He penetrated even to the straits (of Aden). To the north he subdued the Bejas, the nomad tribes who inhabit the desert behind Suakim. To the north-west he subdued the Tangaites 'who dwell up to the bounds of Egypt' and caused a road to be constructed from his own kingdom as far as Egypt. Finally he crossed the sea and conquered the peoples of the Arrabites and Kinaedocolpites, who probably occupied the Hejjaz, and compelled their kings to pay him tribute and to guarantee the security of the trade routes both by land and by sea. He concludes:

'Of the kings that went before me I am the first and only one to have subdued all these peoples by the grace granted to me by my mighty god Ares, who also begat me. It is through him that I have subdued all the peoples that border upon my empire, to the east as far as the land of perfumes, to the west as far as the land of Ethiopia[1] and Sasu. Some I fought myself, against others I sent my armies. When I had established peace in the lands subject to me I came to Adulis to sacrifice on behalf of those who voyage on the sea to Zeus, Ares, and Poseidon. Having assembled all my armies I have set up here this throne and have consecrated it to Ares in the twenty-seventh year of my reign.'

After making due allowance for royal braggadocio, it is nevertheless evident that this king was a great conqueror and may justly be styled the founder of the Abyssinian Empire. Unfortunately, the beginning of the inscription was missing when Cosmas saw it, or at any rate Cosmas did not transcribe it. The name and date of the king are thus unknown. By internal evidence the date may be fixed to the third century A.D. The name of the king may be Aphilas. Aphilas was at any rate an important Axumite king of this period; many of his coins are extant.

The next king of Axum of whom we have any information is Aeizanas, son of Ella Amida, who reigned in the second quarter of the fourth century. This king has made known his exploits to posterity in a series of inscriptions, one in Greek, Ge'ez, and Sabaean (the language of Yemen), one in Sabaean, the rest in Ge'ez. These inscriptions thus reveal a native culture growing up beside the imported culture of Greece. In his royal protocol he styles himself 'king of Axum, Himyar, Raidan, Saba, Salhin, Siamo, Bega, and Kasu, king of kings, son of the unconquered Mahrem (in Greek Ares)'. The mention of Saba and Himyar shows that since the days of Aphilas (?) the Abyssinian Empire had been enlarged to include Yemen. It is less certain that Aeizanas actually ruled south-western Arabia. His campaigns are all in Africa. The trilingual inscription records

---

[1] It may be noted that the king of Axum regards Ethiopia as a foreign country at this period. Ethiopia designates Nubia.

HISTORICAL ORIGIN

the suppression of a revolt of the Bejas by the king's brothers Sazanas and Hadefan. The other inscriptions mostly record campaigns against unknown peoples. The last, which relates a series of campaigns against the Nubians, is of more interest.

The Nubians, according to the king, had shown a haughty and rebellious spirit. They had said in their hearts: 'They will not dare to cross the Takazzé'; they had attacked their neighbours; the black people had fought against the red. Finally, when Aeizanas had sent envoys to reprove them, they had insulted and robbed them. Provoked by this insolence, Aeizanas resolved on a punitive expedition. He won a battle at a ford of the Takazzé and pursued the fugitives westward to the Seda (Blue Nile), where many of them were drowned. He destroyed their towns, both those built of stone and those of thatch, and burned their stores of corn and cotton.[1] He then marched down the Blue Nile into the land of the Red Nubians and subdued them also. The distinction drawn in the inscription between the red people and the black is interesting. The former are the original Hamitic population who built up the Meroitic civilization. The latter are the Nilotic negroes who were already filtering into these regions. In northern Nubia the original population was apparently still undisturbed. In the south the two populations lived side by side, the civilized Hamites in stone-built towns, the negroes in their thatch villages.

The inscription has a greater interest than this. It is the first Christian document of Abyssinia.

[1] Cotton is probably indigenous in the Sudan and has been cultivated from time immemorial.

v. THE CONVERSION OF THE KINGDOM

The story of the evangelization of Abyssinia is thus told by Rufinus:

'One Metrodorus, a philosopher, is said to have penetrated to further India in order to view places and see the world. Inspired by his example, one Meropius, a philosopher of Tyre, wished to visit India with a similar object, taking with him two small boys who were related to him and whom he was educating in humane studies. The younger of these was called Aedesius, the other Frumentius. When, having seen and taken note of what his soul fed upon, the philosopher had begun to return, the ship on which he travelled put in for water or some other necessary at a certain port. It is the custom of the barbarians of these parts that, if ever the neighbouring tribes report that their treaty with the Romans is broken, all Romans found among them should be massacred. The philosopher's ship was boarded; all with himself were put to the sword. The boys were found studying under a tree and preparing their lessons, and, preserved by the mercy of the barbarians, were taken to the king. He made one of them, Aedesius, his cupbearer. Frumentius, whom he had perceived to be sagacious and prudent, he made his treasurer and secretary. Thereafter they were held in great honour and affection by the king. The king died, leaving his wife with an infant son as heir of the bereaved kingdom. He gave the young men liberty to do what they pleased but the queen besought them with tears, since she had no more faithful subjects in the whole kingdom, to share with her the cares of governing the kingdom until her son should grow up, especially Frumentius, whose ability was equal to guiding the kingdom—for the other, though loyal and honest of heart, was simple. While they lived there and Frumentius held the reins of government in his hands, God stirred up his heart and he began to search out with care those of the Roman merchants who were Christians and to give them great influence and to urge them to establish in various places conventicles to which

THE CONVERSION 27

they might resort for prayer in the Roman manner. He himself, moreover, did the same and so encouraged the others, attracting them with his favour and his benefits, providing them with whatever was needed, supplying sites for buildings and other necessaries, and in every way promoting the growth of the seed of Christianity in the country. When the prince for whom they exercised the regency had grown up, they completed and faithfully delivered over their trust, and, though the queen and her son sought greatly to detain them and begged them to remain, returned to the Roman Empire. Aedesius hastened to Tyre to revisit his parents and relatives. Frumentius went to Alexandria, saying that it was not right to hide the work of God. He laid the whole affair before the bishop and urged him to look for some worthy man to send as bishop over the many Christians already congregated and the churches built on barbarian soil. Then Athanasius (for he had recently assumed the episcopate), having carefully weighed and considered Frumentius' words and deeds, declared in a council of the priests: "What other man shall we find in whom the Spirit of God is as in thee, who can accomplish these things?" And he consecrated him and bade him return in the grace of God whence he had come. And when he had arrived in India as bishop, such grace is said to have been given to him by God that apostolic miracles were wrought by him and a countless number of barbarians were converted by him to the faith. From which time Christian peoples and churches have been created in the parts of India, and the priesthood has begun. These facts I know not from vulgar report but from the mouth of Aedesius himself, who had been Frumentius' companion and was later made a priest in Tyre.'

There is no doubt that this romantic story is authentic, for Rufinus lived in the latter part of the fourth century and may well have spoken with Aedesius, then an old man. The story is, moreover, supported by other pieces of evidence which prove that Rufinus' 'India' is Abyssinia, and that the king who took Frumentius and Aedesius into his service

THE CONVERSION

was Ella Amida, and that the prince for whom they executed the regency was Aeizanas. The first confirmatory piece of evidence is a letter, cited by Athanasius, directed by the emperor Constantius to 'his most precious brothers' Aeizanas and Sazanas (who it may be recalled is mentioned in Aeizanas' trilingual inscription), dynasts of the Axumites. Frumentius, it will be remembered, had been consecrated by Athanasius, the champion of the Nicene faith, shortly after he became patriarch of Alexandria in 328. Since that date the tide had turned in ecclesiastical affairs; the Arian faith now triumphed under the patronage of Constantius and Athanasius had been expelled from the chair of Alexandria. The object of Constantius' letter is to urge Aeizanas to send Frumentius to Alexandria to be examined in the faith by George of Cappadocia, who supplanted Athanasius as patriarch of Alexandria in A.D. 356. The emperor's attempt to make Frumentius subscribe to the Arian faith does not seem to have been successful.

The second piece of evidence is the already mentioned inscription of Aeizanas commemorating the conquest of the Nubians. In this inscription he no longer styles himself 'son of the unconquered Mahrem' but simply 'son of Ella Amida, the unconquered', and he attributes his victories, not as heretofore, to his tutelary god Mahrem, but to 'the Lord of the Heavens who has power over all beings in heaven and earth'. This phrase is not perhaps quite explicit evidence of Christianity, but the coins of Aeizanas show that it is to be interpreted in a Christian sense. His early coins bear the pagan symbol of the crescent and the disk, his later coins bear the cross. It appears then that Frumentius, on his return to Axum as bishop, succeeded in converting the king to Christianity, not immediately, for the majority of Aeizanas' inscriptions and coins are pagan, but towards the end of his reign. The fact that this, Frumentius' crowning achievement, is not mentioned in Rufinus' story is good evidence of its authenticity. Aedesius, Rufinus' informant, could tell him of the part of Frumentius' career which he himself had witnessed; of his later evangelical work he had only the vaguest reports.

The Abyssinian story of their own conversion agrees substantially with Rufinus' account. A slight difficulty is caused in the Abyssinian account by the fact that they have applied to themselves, with all the other biblical references to Ethiopia, the famous story of Philip and the eunuch. Queen Candace as a matter of fact ruled in Meroe and was queen of Nubia and not of Abyssinia. The author of Acts, furthermore, never states that she was converted, and in point of fact Nubia remained pagan some two centuries after Abyssinia was converted. Abyssinian tradition, however, asserted that the eunuch whom Philip baptized had evangelized Abyssinia in the apostolic age. This was embarrassing, for it left Frumentius very little to do. The difficulty was successfully circumvented. The Abyssinians, it appears, received the true faith from the eunuch of Queen Candace, but, since he had never been consecrated bishop, they lacked the priesthood and the sacraments. Frumentius, or as he is more commonly called in the Abyssinian stories, Abba Salama (the father of peace), finding them already orthodox, had only to introduce to them the sacraments.

There is a second discrepancy in the Abyssinian version of the story. It knows nothing of Aeizanas, but makes two twin brothers, Atsbeha and Abraha, the first Christian kings of Ethiopia. In so doing Abyssinian tradition follows a very common tendency of popular history to attach famous events to famous names. For Atsbeha and Abraha were renowned champions of the Christian faith, but they flourished two centuries later than Aeizanas. The authentic story of these 'twin brothers' is as follows:

Ella Atsbeha, or as the Greeks called him Ellesbaas or Ellestheaeus, also known as Kaleb, reigned in Abyssinia in the second quarter of the sixth century. At this time Judaism had acquired great influence in Yemen and a Jewish king reigned over Himyar. This king began a great persecution of the Christians in his kingdom and massacred vast numbers of them. Ellesbaas then arose as champion of the Christians—and incidentally of the lapsed suzerain rights of the kings of Axum over south-western Arabia. In the reign of Justin, about A.D. 525, he dispatched a great expedition to Himyar, the preparations for which were witnessed by Cosmas during that visit to Adulis when he copied the two inscriptions. The expedition was completely successful, and Ellesbaas set up as tributary king of Himyar one Esimphaeus, a Christian Himyarite. A few years later the Abyssinian army of occupation in Himyar revolted against Esimphaeus and set up as king one Abraham, a Christian, formerly the slave of a Roman resident in Adulis. Ellesbaas sent two expeditions against Abraham, one of which went over to his side and the other was completely defeated. Discouraged by his reverses, Ellesbaas recognized Abraham, who on his side acknowledged the suzerainty of Ellesbaas and paid him tribute. Ellesbaas won great renown by his suppression of the Jewish king of Himyar. In the *Kebra Nagast* this event is reckoned as the final catastrophe of the kingdom of Judah. Abraham also won great fame as a champion of Christianity. He built a magnificent church in Sana'a, his capital, which excited the wonder of the Arabs and bade fair to eclipse the Ka'aba at Mecca as a centre of pilgrimage. He even proposed to destroy the Ka'aba. This expedition plays a great part in the traditions of Islam. He is said to have marched against

Mecca mounted on a mighty elephant and followed by a vast host. But God intervened to save the Ka'aba, which was destined to have so glorious a history. A flight of birds appeared over the army and dropped small stones upon it, and, where the soldiers were struck by the stones, pustules broke out and they sickened and died. It was in the Year of the Elephant, according to Moslem tradition, that the Prophet was born.

These two great champions of the Christian faith, about whom a maze of legends has gathered in Abyssinian and Arabic tradition, became eventually the twin brothers who introduced Christianity into Abyssinia.

vi. THE CIVILIZATION OF THE PRIMITIVE KINGDOM

Of Abyssinian civilization at this period we have only a few tantalizing glimpses. Cosmas gives a curious picture of the commercial relations of the Abyssinians with the interior in the sixth century A.D. Every other year, he says, the king of the Axumites sends through the governor of Agau (by which is presumably meant the Hamitic peoples on the southern edge of the kingdom around Lake Tsana) special agents to the land of Sasu, where gold is mined. These agents are accompanied by a large number of merchants, more than five hundred, and the caravan takes with it cattle and bars of salt and iron. When they reach the borders of Sasu they pitch a camp and fence it with a great hedge of thorns, and on the hedge they lay the bars of salt and iron and pieces of meat. Presently the natives arrive and lay nuggets of gold, the size of beans, on the objects which they want to buy, and then retire. If the merchant is satisfied with the price offered he removes the gold, and the purchaser then removes the meat or salt or iron. If the merchant is dissatisfied he leaves the gold and waits for the purchaser to add more, if he still wishes to buy, or to take away his gold if he thinks the price too high. The haggling generally takes about five days, the whole expedition about six months. The caravan travels well armed for fear of being robbed by the savage tribes through whose territory it passes. On its outward journey it has to move slowly on account of the cattle, on its homeward way it travels as fast as it can for fear of being caught by the rains.

We also possess a brief description of the Abyssinian court in the sixth century A.D. The emperor Justinian sent an ambassador, a certain Julian, to Ellesbaas with the object of developing trade connexions with India via Abyssinia. The Roman Empire imported large quantities of silk from India, whither it was brought from China, and this trade had hitherto passed through the Persian Empire via the Persian Gulf and Mesopotamia. Justinian was at war with the Persian king and had no desire to enrich him with the profits of this trade, and he conceived the idea that the Abyssinian kingdom, a friendly Christian power, might open direct communication by sea with India and so cut out the Persians. The scheme miscarried, for the Abyssinians did not venture farther than the ports of the Persian Gulf, and there they were naturally unable to break the monopoly of the Persian merchants, who bought every Indian cargo directly it arrived. But Julian, the ambassador of Justinian, wrote a description of the Abyssinian court of which a fragment has survived. The king, he wrote, was naked, wearing only a garment of linen embroidered with gold from his waist to his loins and straps set with pearls over his back and stomach. He wore golden bracelets on his arms, and on his head a turban of linen embroidered with gold from which hung four fillets on either side; around his neck was a golden collar. He stood on a four-wheeled chariot drawn by four elephants; the body of the chariot was high and covered with gold plates. The king stood on top carrying a small gilded shield and holding in his hands two small gilded spears. His council stood around similarly armed and flutes played. Julian, on being introduced, knelt and made obeisance, but the king bade him rise. He was brought forward and presented the emperor's letter. The king kissed the seal and expressed great pleasure at the gifts which were produced. Then he opened the letter and it was read to him by an interpreter.

This picture of the barbaric splendour of the early kings of Axum accords well with the only material relic they have left behind them, the so-called obelisks of Axum. The largest of these gigantic granite monoliths surpass in size the largest obelisks of Egypt. Their purpose is unknown, for they are uninscribed; they may, like the obelisks of Egypt, be dedicated to a god of the sky; they may be funerary monuments of kings. The origin of their form is equally obscure. Though superficially they resemble the Egyptian obelisks and may owe their inspiration partly to them, they differ from them in many important details. They are oblong and not square in plan, and the most highly finished examples terminate not in a pyramidal cap but in a crescent and disk, a religious symbol familiar from the coinage of the Axumite kings. Their decoration is most peculiar. It consists of an imitation door at the bottom and above it several tiers of imitation windows, separated by imitation log floors. They are in fact models of towers, cut out of a single block of stone, and seem to represent a fusion of the monolithic funerary stelae characteristic of Arabia and the tomb towers of which those of Palmyra are the most famous. But whatever their purpose and origin they are an impressive testimony to the magnificence of the last pagan and first Christian kings of Abyssinia.

During the first six centuries of its existence the indigenous culture of the Abyssinian kingdom was steadily developing and ousting the imported culture of Greece. The first king of whom we know had a Greek education; his successors in the third century used Greek as the official language of their public documents. In the fourth century Ge'ez was supplanting Greek as an official language, and the knowledge of Greek was probably declining. This would explain the rapid rise of Frumentius in the royal service; Ella Amida must have found a young man who had received a Greek literary education very useful to conduct his diplomatic correspondence. By the sixth century the governor of Adulis knew no Greek, since he had to call upon a passing Roman merchant to read the Greek inscriptions of Ptolemy III and Aphilas (?). Ellesbaas himself seems to have known no Greek; he used an interpreter to read Justinian's letter. The coins continue to bear Greek legends in his reign and even later, but coins are always conservative, especially among backward peoples, who will only accept a familiar type; the early caliphs had to issue copies of Byzantine coins, charged with the cross, and in Abyssinia copies of Maria Theresa dollars were the only currency down to the end of the last century and are still widely used.

The primitive language of the Abyssinian Church was, it may be presumed, Greek, since its nucleus was formed by Roman merchants resident in the country. The liturgy and the scriptures were first translated into Ge'ez in the latter part of the fifth century, when, presumably, the number of native converts was becoming considerable. The translators were a group of holy men celebrated in Abyssinian legend as the Nine Saints. They seem to have been learned monks who migrated from Syria. The Ge'ez version of the New Testament is not, as might have been

The Obelisks of Axum

expected, based on the Alexandrian text, but on that of Antioch. One of the sacred works which the Nine Saints introduced, the *Kerlos*, a Christological treatise formed of extracts from the Fathers, mostly from Cyril himself, is also probably of Syrian origin. It is a confutation of Nestorianism, which never penetrated Abyssinia and had no influence in Egypt, but was a dangerous rival of the orthodox and monophysite faiths in Syria. The Nine Saints are credited with having introduced monastic institutions into Abyssinia; another of their translations is the Rule of Pachomius, the founder of Eastern monasticism. The version of the scriptures which they gave to the Abyssinian Church is of high interest to us, since it contains several apocryphal works current in the fifth and sixth centuries, the originals of which have since perished; thus the Books of Enoch and Jubilees are known to us—in their entirety—only through the Ge'ez version. The translations made by this school include only one work of secular learning, the *Physiologus*, a pseudo-scientific treatise. These works formed for centuries the whole literature of Abyssinia.

vii. THE ABYSSINIAN CHURCH

Frumentius, the first bishop of Axum, was consecrated by Athanasius, patriarch of Alexandria. Ever since that day the head of the Abyssinian Church has, with hardly an exception, been nominated by the head of the Egyptian Church. The Alexandrian patriarchate has, from its inception, possessed a far more centralized structure than the other Eastern patriarchates. Throughout Egypt the patriarch alone has, and always has had, the right of consecrating bishops; his metropolitans exercise only a delegated authority and are not, as elsewhere in the East, independent within their own provinces. The same policy of centralization which prevailed in Egypt was applied to the outlying province of Abyssinia. The head of the Abyssinian Church, though he bears the exalted title of Catholicus, second only in dignity to Patriarch, has always been a nominee of the patriarch of Alexandria and has strictly limited prerogatives in his own province. In order that there may be no doubt in this question the Copts have forged a canon of the Council of Nicaea—which incidentally was held some years before the Abyssinian Church existed—in which it is specifically laid down that the Ethiopians shall not choose their own Catholicus, but that he shall be appointed by the patriarch of Alexandria, and that, though in honour he is like a patriarch, he has no patriarchal power, in particular he cannot appoint metropolitans. The apocryphal canon also provides that, in the unlikely contingency of an oecumenical council being held under the presidency of the patriarch of Rome, the Catholicus of Ethiopia shall be ninth in order of precedence among the bishops of all Christendom. The prerogatives of the Catholicus, or, as he is usually called, the Abuna (our father), in Abyssinia are somewhat obscure. In point of fact he seems during the greater part of Abyssinian history to have been the only bishop in the country. He had, however, in earlier times the power of consecrating bishops up to the number of seven. The number of bishops was limited lest they should, in defiance of the apocryphal canon of Nicaea, elect their own catholicus; twelve bishops are required by Coptic canon law for this purpose.

The Abyssinian Church, being so closely dependent on that of Egypt, has naturally followed its lead implicitly on doctrinal questions. When Frumentius was appointed, the patriarchate of Alexandria, under the leadership of Athanasius, was the stronghold of the Nicene faith against

Arianism. During the Arian reaction which took place under Constantius, Athanasius was expelled and an intruder, George of Cappadocia, put in his place, but Egypt as a whole held by Athanasius and the Nicene faith, and Abyssinia seems to have followed suit. Constantius sent a letter to Aeizanas, urging him to send Frumentius to receive instruction from George, but apparently without effect. He later sent one Theophilus, a native of Socotra, to preach Arianism in Himyar and Saba and Abyssinia. Philostorgius, an Arian historian, recounts his triumph in Himyar and Saba, but from his guarded reference to Abyssinia it may be inferred that Theophilus was not successful there. On the accession of Theodosius I the faith of Nicaea, as taught by the bishops of Rome and Alexandria, was finally recognized as orthodox. The patriarchs of Alexandria continued to be champions of orthodoxy, combating the Macedonian and Apollinarian heresies, which were condemned at the Council of Constantinople in A.D. 381, and Nestorianism, which was condemned at the Council of Ephesus in A.D. 431. But leaning from Nestorianism too strongly, they toppled off the narrow path of orthodoxy. So anxious were they to refute the Nestorian view that the man Christ was clothed with the Godhead as with a garment that they asserted that the manhood of Christ was absorbed in his divinity. This view that Christ had one nature was condemned by the Council of Chalcedon in A.D. 451, which laid down that there were two natures, one human, one divine, in Christ. The Chalcedonian faith, which both the Western Churches and the Greek Orthodox Church of the East hold, has never been accepted by the Church of Alexandria. In the years that followed Chalcedon there was a prolonged struggle between the Roman government, which was generally Chalcedonian, and the people of Egypt, which was stubbornly monophysite. From time to time Chalcedonian patriarchs were enthroned at Alexandria by armed force, but they never commanded the allegiance of the clergy and people. Eventually under Justinian there was a definite schism, and a monophysite Egyptian (Coptic) patriarch ruled side by side with a Chalcedonian imperialist (Melkite) patriarch. There can be little doubt which side the Abyssinian Church took in this struggle. One of its earliest sacred books, the *Kerlos*, has a distinctly monophysite flavour, and there can be little doubt that the Nine Saints who brought it with them from Syria were monophysite confessors expelled from Syria, another stronghold of the monophysite faith, after Chalcedon. Certainly ever since the Arab conquest of Egypt, which was the death-blow of the Melkite cause in that country, the Abyssinian Church has shared the monophysite faith of the Coptic Church.

In its ritual, calendar, and customs the Abyssinian Church naturally follows the Coptic. Their liturgy follows the rite of St. Mark. They observe the very long and numerous fasts of Copts, who have, among other things, added ten extra days to Lent. Like the Copts they celebrate the anniversary of our Lord's Baptism (Epiphany) with ritual bathing. They reckon their years from the Era of the Martyrs. They use the Coptic calendar—which is the ancient Egyptian modified by the insertion of an extra day at Leap Year and has twelve months of thirty days each and five (or six) extra days. The Abyssinian Church has, however, many peculiar features. Some of these are survivals of paganism. Such are the barbaric dances and the beating of drums which enliven the liturgy on solemn occasions. Such again was the ancient practice, given canonical sanction by the Coptic patriarch in the ninth century, of sacrificing an ox, a ewe and a she-goat on the dedication of a church. The curious practice of

THE ABYSSINIAN CHURCH

celebrating certain feasts, the Nativity, Our Lady, St. Michael, and Abraham, Isaac, and Jacob, once a month is also probably a concession to the pagan semitic calendar, which was strictly lunar. Other Abyssinian peculiarities have a curiously Jewish appearance. That they circumcise is of no significance; circumcision is by no means a peculiarly Jewish custom, being followed not only by the Moslems but also by the Copts, and it is a purely social custom in Abyssinia, celebrated by no religious ritual. It is, however, rather odd that the Abyssinians observe the Mosaic distinction between clean and unclean meat, rejecting the flesh of beasts that do not chew the cud and cleave the hoof or have been torn or strangled, that they regard those who have had sexual intercourse as impure for the following day, refusing them access to their churches, and furthermore that they observe the Sabbath as well as Sunday, celebrating the liturgy on both days alike and exempting both days from fasts.

If one could accept the national legend of Solomon and the Queen of the South as historical, these Judaisms would be simply explained. The Abyssinians, according to their own story, practised the law of Moses from the reign of Menelik onwards and clung to those remnants of the Mosaic law after their conversion to Christianity. The real explanation is uncertain. In part the Judaizing tendency of Abyssinian Christianity may be due to an uncritical reverence for the Old Testament. In modern Europe an intensive study of the scriptures, unguided by the tradition of the Church, has produced a markedly Judaic tone in some of the extremer Protestant Churches. The Abyssinians have considerably more excuse if they developed their religion on the same lines to more exaggerated degree. They were a people of Semitic culture, and many parts of the Mosaic law, embodying as they do the common heritage of the Semitic peoples, did not seem strange to them. They were never in close touch with the main body of the Church and only three centuries after their first evangelization were almost completely cut off from it, and left to study the holy books which had been delivered to them without any outside guidance. In these circumstances it is little wonder if they adopted various ceremonial laws which were laid down in the holy books and were, moreover, in accord with their cultural tradition. Some, at any rate, of their Jewish practices are, it may be noted, obviously conscious adaptations of the Mosaic law to Christian practice. Infants are, for instance, baptized on the fortieth day if males, or the eightieth if females, the Christian rite of baptism being governed by the Mosaic regulations on presentation at the Temple.

This is not, however, the whole explanation. The Jewish customs of the Abyssinians—which it may be noted cannot be traced farther back than the Middle Ages—might be thus explained. There still remains the curious circumstance that a number of Abyssinian words connected with religion—Hell, idol, Easter, purification, alms—are of Hebrew origin. These words must have been derived directly from a Jewish source, for the Abyssinian Church knows the scriptures only in a Ge'ez version made from the Septuagint. There remains also that curious enigma, the black Jews of Abyssinia. The Falashas (exiles), as they are called by the Abyssinians, are not scattered individuals. They are a people, or were so until comparatively recent times. Their home is Semien, the very mountainous country north of Lake Tsana, where they used to live under their own kings. They are certainly not Jews by race. They are of the indigenous Agau stock of Abyssinia and speak a Hamitic language. They know no Hebrew, and their scriptures are the Ge'ez version of the Old Testa-

THE ABYSSINIAN CHURCH

ment. Their Judaism is of a curiously archaic type. They do not possess the Mishna or the Talmud, and they do not observe the feast of Purim, nor do they celebrate the dedication or the destruction of the second temple. On the other hand, their customs are contaminated by Christian influence. They have, for instance, a monastic system, introduced according to their own traditions in the fourth century A.D., and their priests, according to the custom of the Eastern Church, must marry once only. They are first mentioned in the works of Eldad the Danite, a Jewish traveller of the ninth century A.D., who was something of a romancer but seems to have picked up some genuine information about the obscurer Jewish communities of Africa and Asia. Eldad states that the Jews of Abyssinia are a portion of the Ten Tribes. Their own tradition agrees with that of Christian Abyssinia. They profess to be descended from the Israelites who accompanied Menelik on his return from the court of Solomon, and they traced their royal line back to Menelik. Some modern scholars have proposed to derive the Falashas from the Jewish colonies which are known to have existed in Upper Egypt in the fifth century B.C. and were probably formed by emigrants from Palestine after the destruction of Jerusalem by Nebuchadnezzar. This theory is as untenable as those of Eldad the Danite and of the Falashas themselves, for the Judaism of the colonies of Upper Egypt was highly unorthodox, as the Aramaic papyri of Assouan have proved, whereas the Judaism of the Falashas is of the normal post-exilic type.

The true explanation both of the Falashas and of the Hebrew words in Abyssinian probably lies in the strong Jewish influence which prevailed in the Hejjaz and Yemen in the centuries which preceded the rise of Islam. When Judaism began to propagate itself in these countries is uncertain, but it is probable that many Jews migrated beyond the bounds of the Roman Empire into south-western Arabia after the destruction of Jerusalem by Titus and again after the suppression of the revolt of Barcochbar by Hadrian. It is at any rate certain that in the sixth and early seventh centuries Jews swarmed in the Hejjaz and Yemen and that, moreover, a great movement of proselytism had taken place and was still in progress. The traditions of pre-Islamic Arabia are full of allusion to Jewish tribes and kingdoms, and it may be recalled that a Jewish king of Himyar was crushed by Ellesbaas early in the sixth century. It is a plausible conjecture that in Abyssinia, which had at this period very close commercial and political relations with south-western Arabia and was, moreover, closely akin to it in language and culture, similar conditions may have prevailed, and Judaism may have been competing with Christianity to convert the heathen and may perhaps have had an earlier start. The conversion of the royal house to Christianity by Frumentius prevented Judaism from becoming the official religion of the Abyssinian kingdom, but was not in time to prevent the conversion of various independent Agau tribes to Judaism nor the adoption by the Abyssinians of certain Jewish practices.

Abyssinian Christianity is, then, at base the Coptic Christianity of Egypt contaminated by a number of pagan survivals and by certain Jewish elements introduced concurrently with or even before Christianity. Its many peculiarities are due in part to these contaminations, but for the most part to the isolation in which it developed. Unguided by the tradition of the Church, it struck out an eccentric line of growth inspired by an uncritical study of the scriptures. To similar causes is also in all probability to be attributed the archaic character of Falasha Judaism. The illiterate Agau tribes which adopted Judaism if they

THE ABYSSINIAN CHURCH

ever learned Hebrew must soon have forgotten it, and if ever they possessed any Hebrew books must soon have ceased to be able to read them. They had to rely on such sacred books as existed in the literary language of the country, Ge'ez, that is, on the Ge'ez version of the Old Testament made for the Abyssinian Church.[1] Thus, when the connexions with the rest of Jewry were broken and the tradition handed down from the first missionaries grew more and more dim, they fell back on the written word and their religious institutions assumed a strongly archaistic and Mosaic character. Some traditional elements survived; for though they do not possess the Talmud, some of their customs show Talmudic influence. Certain Christian customs also were borrowed from their neighbours.

[1] According to Bruce, the Falashas in his day (1770–72) bought their copies of the Old Testament from the Christians, having no scribes of their own.

PART II

i. THE DARK AGE OF ABYSSINIA

THE rise of Islam was the turning-point in the history of Abyssinia. Hitherto, though a remote and barbaric kingdom, Abyssinia had lain upon the fringe of a kindred and friendly civilization. The Roman emperors might persecute monophysites within the empire. Beyond its boundaries they were the champions of Christianity of any form against the Zoroastrian empire of Persia and its pagan and Jewish allies; even that fanatical persecutor Justinian maintained the friendliest relations with Ellesbaas. Had it remained within the orbit of the Christian civilization of Byzantium, Abyssinian culture might have developed on much less eccentric lines. But it is idle to conjecture what might have happened. In 636 the Arab armies occupied Palestine and Syria, in 640–2 they occupied Egypt. Henceforth the Christian kingdoms of Abyssinia and Nubia were cut off from the Christian Empire of Rome. From this time the history of Abyssinia is plunged in the deepest obscurity, illumined dimly by passing references in the history of the Coptic Patriarchs and rare allusions in the Arab historians and geographers. It is not until the end of the thirteenth century that native Abyssinian chronicles emerge from the dim regions of legend and begin to assume an historical character, and it is only in the sixteenth century, with the arrival of the Portuguese, that we obtain any comprehensive view of the development of Abyssinian civilization.

The first contacts of Abyssinia with the infant power of Islam were not unfriendly. The king of Abyssinia afforded a refuge at his court for the exiled adherents of the new prophet in their first struggles with the pagan aristocracy of Mecca. The king of Abyssinia was, according to Moslem tradition, the only one among the kings of the earth to whom Mohammed announced his mission who sent a reply. He is said to have received the prophet's letter with reverence and to have expressed approval of his teaching. The historical value of the tradition is very questionable. The first reactions of the Abyssinian king may, however, have been favourable to the new prophet. He at any rate aimed at the destruction of paganism in Arabia and his letter to the Abyssinian king, as given by the Arab historians, diplomatically emphasizes his reverence for Jesus and Mary. Be that as it may, when the Abyssinians realized the true character of the new doctrine, they rejected it. But their early kindness to the prophet and his followers bore some fruit. Arabic writers of the tenth century declare that, Christians though they are, there is no jihad (holy war) against the Abyssinians.

Despite this fact the relations of Abyssinia to the early caliphs were not always friendly. The Abyssinians at this period took to piracy on a large scale. Their fleets ravaged the commerce of the Red Sea. They made frequent descents upon the coasts of Arabia. In 702 they even sacked Jidda, the port of Mecca, and there was an alarming prophecy current that one day they would capture Mecca itself and destroy the Ka'aba. The caliphs retorted by occupying the ports of Abyssinia which were the bases of the pirate fleets. There is a story that in 634 Omar banished a man to Massaua; it appears then that as early as this one of the principal Abyssinian ports was in the possession of the Arabs. This occupation can, however, have been temporary only, for the raids of the Abyssinians were at their worst some seventy years later. It was not until the early eighth century, after the famous sack of Jidda, that the Arabic occupation of the Abyssinian coast became effective. In the paintings which adorn the walls of the palace which Walid (705–15) built for himself at Quseir Amra, the Negus figures beside Caesar, Chosroes (a Persian pretender), and Roderic (the last Visigothic king of Spain) among the kings whom the caliph had subdued. Walid's boast does not seem to have been vain, for a few years later the islands of Dahlak off the Abyssinian coast are found in Arab occupation and Abyssinian piracy is heard of no more. It was about this period that Adulis was destroyed, never to rise again.

With the loss of its Red Sea ports the Abyssinian kingdom was completely cut off from access to the civilized world. During the next two centuries its energies seem to have been directed southwards. In the hagiographical writings of Abyssinia there are preserved dim records of the holy men who, during this period, evangelized Amhara and Shoa. While the Abyssinian kingdom was thus recruiting its forces the hold of the caliphs on the coast had been relaxed. Pagan Beja tribes, later converted to Islam, occupied the coastal parts of Tigré, and Dahlak passed under the sway of tribes from Yemen. Towards the end of the ninth century the Abyssinian kings seem to have succeeded in reconquering the ancient coastal dominions. At the beginning of the tenth century Abyssinia was once again a maritime and commercial power, in friendly relations with the kingdom of Yemen. It owned Massaua and Dahlak, whose Moslem inhabitants paid tribute to the Abyssinian king, and it had, moreover, acquired a new outlet to the sea far to the south at Zeila; this also was a Moslem town, but tributary to the Abyssinian king.

In about 975 Abyssinia was still flourishing. Shortly after this a dramatic reversal of fortune occurred. The story is thus told in the *History of the Patriarchs of Alexandria*. Towards the end of the tenth century the king of

Abyssinia wrote to George, king of Nubia. He was in distress. A queen was ravaging his country, enslaving his people, burning the churches, and chasing him and his few remaining followers from refuge to refuge. The clergy were being slaughtered, the Christian religion was in danger of perishing. These disasters he attributed to the breach, now of long standing, between the court of Abyssinia and the patriarchate of Alexandria. Its origin lay back at the beginning of the century, when an Abyssinian king had on his death-bed entrusted to the then abuna, Peter, the task of choosing which of his two sons should be king. Peter had chosen the younger. But presently two Egyptian monks, Minas and Victor, had appeared on the scene and produced a forged letter from the patriarch declaring that Peter was an impostor and that Minas, with Victor as his assistant, was the true abuna, and furthermore that Peter's choice of the younger son was illegal. The elder son, thus encouraged, expelled his brother and Peter, and acknowledged Minas as abuna. Not long after, however, Victor fell out with his accomplice and having sacked his house fled to Egypt with his ill-gotten gains, which he spent on riotous living. The intrigue thus came to light. The king executed Minas and sought for Peter, but in vain, for he had died in exile. He then asked the patriarch for a new abuna, but he, incensed at the treatment which Peter had received, refused, and his four successors maintained the refusal. The king, driven to desperation, forced Peter's assistant to exercise the function of abuna without the consecration of the patriarch. It was to these events that the king who wrote to George of Nubia attributed his misfortunes, and he begged George to use his influence with the patriarch of Alexandria to induce him to relent and to send him a canonically ordained abuna.

The name of the country over which the queen reigned

is unfortunately corrupt in the Arabic text. It is plain, however, that she was not a Christian, and the most plausible emendation is Damot, a kingdom within the loop of the Abai where paganism long flourished and where, according to tradition, the government was in the hands of women. The disaster which overwhelmed the Abyssinian kingdom at this date was then a resurgence of the indigenous pagan Agau peoples of the central highlands. According to the *History of the Patriarchs*, George's entreaties were successful, the patriarch sent a new abuna, and the queen was promptly subdued. But, even if the divine favour manifested itself so rapidly, the power of the Abyssinian kings had been severely shaken and their outlying possessions fell away. From about this time an independent Moslem dynasty began to rule in Dahlak. Zeila was also lost to Abyssinia and Islam began to make great progress in the adjacent parts of northern Somaliland, where a number of Moslem kingdoms arose which were to be among the most dangerous enemies of Abyssinia.

About 1150 an embassy arrived in Cairo from the king of Abyssinia to ask the patriarch for a new abuna. It was alleged that the old abuna, Michel, was so decrepit that he could not perform his functions. The actual fact was that the king was a usurper and that Michel had refused to acknowledge him. The patriarch, aware of the true state of affairs, declared that it was uncanonical to consecrate another abuna while the old one still lived and persisted in his refusal despite pressure from the vizier. The usurping king in this story is fairly certainly the founder of the Zagué dynasty, which according to the best Abyssinian tradition reigned for one hundred and thirty-three years and was certainly overthrown in about A.D. 1270. The Zagué dynasty seems to mark a reaction of the Agau element against the dominant Semitic aristocracy. The home of the dynasty was in Lasta, long a stronghold of the Agaus, and many of its kings have Hamitic names. They were, however, Semitic in culture. Their official language was Ge'ez. They claimed, like the old dynasty, to be of Israelite stock, tracing their descent from Moses instead of Solomon. They were, moreover, pious Christians. One of their number, Lalibala, was particularly noted for his piety and, though he belongs to a dynasty whose memory is condemned in the annals of Ethiopia, has been canonized by the Abyssinian Church. He founded and endowed many churches and monasteries, especially in the southern part of the kingdom, and to him are attributed the most striking monuments of medieval Abyssinia, the rock-hewn churches of Roha, or, as it has been called since his day, Lalibala, the capital of the Zagué dynasty in Lasta. These amazing monuments, of which there are ten, are not mere caverns. Solid blocks of rock have been disengaged from the surrounding plateau by hewing great trenches around them; these blocks have been shaped externally like buildings and hollowed out within. The largest of the churches, that of the Redeemer of the World, measures over a hundred feet long by about seventy-five feet wide. It is surrounded by an external colonnade and the interior is divided into five aisles of eight bays by twenty-eight columns. The others, though not so large, are even more remarkable for their carved ornamentation, which includes curious reliefs of various saints and of the king. The inspiration of these extraordinary churches is unknown. They are said by popular tradition to have been executed by Coptic masons. Their architectural detail shows many traces of Arab and Byzantine influence.

What little other evidence which we possess for the history of Abyssinia during the dark age which extends from the rise of Islam to the restoration of the Solomonian dynasty is concerned with the relations of the Abyssinian Church to the patriarchate of Alexandria. The Moslem conquest of Egypt introduced many difficulties into these relations. The journey from Abyssinia to Egypt was now much more arduous and dangerous than in the days of the Roman Empire, and in times of disturbance the Abyssinian mission was sometimes delayed for many years. The patriarch was now the subject of a Moslem ruler and, as the acknowledged head of the numerous Christian population of Egypt, was often regarded by him with a certain suspicion. This suspicion was heightened by the intimate relations which existed between the patriarch and the courts of the Christian kingdoms which lay to the south of Egypt. Considerable tact and substantial bakshish were needed to allay this suspicion. The Abyssinian king, every time that he required a new abuna, had to placate the court of Cairo with magnificent gifts of ivory and gold and slaves, and the patriarch had to pay an enormous fee for permission to consecrate the new abuna. In the circumstances it is somewhat surprising that the relations between Abyssinia and Egypt were as smooth as they were. But the continued dependence of the Abyssinian Church on the patriarchate of Alexandria was in the interest, real or imaginary, of all parties concerned. The patriarch naturally wished to maintain his prerogatives. The Abyssinian kings feared the wrath of God if they should break the law of the Church. The Moslem rulers of Egypt found an arrangement which gave them an indirect hold over the neighbouring Christian kingdoms not disadvantageous; not only did they gain monetarily from it, but they were able to exercise diplomatic pressure through it and could and did claim counter-concessions—religious freedom for Moslems in Abyssinia, permission for them to erect mosques, and so forth. Only one effort of the Abyssinian kings to shake off the su-

The Church of the Redeemer of the World at Lalibala

Painting from a MS. of King Yekuno Amlak, founder of the restored Solomonian line

premacy of Alexandria is recorded in this period. In the second quarter of the twelfth century the king of Abyssinia brought pressure on the abuna Michel to consecrate more than seven bishops, with the object that they might elect the next abuna. Michel declared that he could not do so without the patriarch's permission, and the king then dispatched a magnificent embassy to the caliph in Cairo to persuade him to bring pressure on the patriarch to consent. The caliph was at first won over to the king's side, but the patriarch eventually convinced him that the ultimate object of the intrigue was to free Abyssinia from the indirect suzerainty of Cairo, and the plan to make the Abyssinian Church autocephalous was thus foiled.

During this period the rule was firmly established, which has prevailed ever since, that the abuna is never an Abyssinian but always an Egyptian, drawn like the other Egyptian bishops from one of the Coptic monasteries. This rule has certain disadvantages. The abuna, whose native language was Coptic or later Arabic, arrived in his province completely ignorant of either Ge'ez, the liturgical language of the Church which he ruled, or Amharic, the language of his flock, and he normally seems to have remained ignorant of them to the end of his days, performing his functions through an interpreter. It was, moreover, often difficult to find a Coptic monk who was willing to face lifelong exile in a remote and barbarous country, and the patriarch was sometimes reduced to sending men not of the highest character, who, as their subsequent careers proved, sought the post only as a means to wealth and power. Despite occasional scandals, however, the Egyptian abunas were on the whole an influence for good. Through them the Abyssinian Church maintained some contact, however slight, with the rest of Christendom. To them and to the patriarchs who sent them were due the periodical efforts at reform in the Abyssinian Church. In the middle of the ninth century the abuna was charged by the patriarch to carry through a thoroughgoing reform. The religious practices of the Abyssinian Church were to be brought into conformity with those of the Egyptian Church; certain concessions were permitted, including the sacrifice of animal victims at the dedication of a church. Above all, polygamy was to be suppressed. The marriage customs of Abyssinia have never been brought into conformity with canon law. Divorce is extremely easy, being permitted for causes stipulated in the marriage contract and being punished only by the payment of damages by the deserting partner. Concubinage is also a regular practice. What the attitude of the Church was in early times is not known, but since the Middle Ages it has, under the inspiration of Alexandria, set its face against these abuses, refusing communion to all who were according to its own canons living in sin. The condemnation of the Church has had very little effect despite successive campaigns by successive abunas. Another struggle against polygamy is recorded towards the end of the eleventh century. It was temporarily successful, even the king being persuaded to dismiss all his wives save the first, but it had no permanent effect.

It is possible that one of the early Zagué kings may have endeavoured to enter into relations with the see of Rome. Our only evidence for this incident is a letter written by Pope Alexander III in 1177 to a monarch whom he styles his 'beloved Son in Christ John, the illustrious and magnificent king of the Indians'. In this letter the Pope states that his physician, Master Philip, has told him that when in the East he met envoys of the king, who informed him that the king was desirous of submitting himself to the Roman see and requested the cession of a church at Rome and an altar in the Church of the Holy Sepulchre at Jerusalem (then under the rule of the Latins). The Pope graciously promises to fulfil these requests if the king will send a regular embassy with a written statement of his proposals. It does not appear that this letter, which was entrusted to Master Philip, ever reached its addressee, and it is evident that the Pope was very vague as to who he was. There can, however, be little doubt that the king, whose envoys had discoursed with Master Philip, was the king of Abyssinia, who was the only Christian king in the Near East who could have sent such an embassy and who, being at the moment at odds with the patriarch of Alexandria, may well have been looking farther afield for a spiritual suzerain. It is known, moreover, that at this period the Abyssinian kings were ambitious to obtain a church at Jerusalem. This ambition was fulfilled ten years later, when Saladin, who had in the meanwhile expelled the Latin kings from the Holy Land, granted to the Abyssinians the chapel of the Invention of the Cross in the Church of the Holy Sepulchre and a station in the grotto of the Nativity in Bethlehem. The Abyssinians have since lost these privileges and have to content themselves with the roof of the chapel of the Invention of the Cross for their devotions.

ii. THE RESTORED SOLOMONIAN LINE

In about 1270 the Zagué dynasty was overthrown by a pretender who claimed descent from the ancient Solomonian line. The restoration of the Solomonian dynasty was marked by a great literary renascence which lasted for some five centuries. Hitherto Abyssinian literature had been confined to the works translated from the Greek by the School of the Nine Saints. The new literature also consisted to a very large extent of translations, from Coptic and Arabic originals. The works translated were for the most part of a religious kind. They include apocryphal stories of Our Lord, his Virgin Mother, and of the Twelve Apostles, chiefly consisting of collections of fantastic miracles. Hagiography plays a very large part. The Synaxar of the Church of Alexandria, a complete calendar of saints for the year, was translated into Ge'ez. Lives of local worthies such as the Zagué king Lalibala and the holy man Takla Haymanot who flourished in the same period, were also written in Ge'ez. There are devotional works, collections of hymns, prayers and litanies, such as the *Praises of Mary* and the *Organ of the Virgin*. There are collections of homilies, some in rhymed prose. There are theological compilations, such as the *Book of Light* and the vast *Faith of the Fathers*. Next in favour to religion comes popular history. To the beginning of the period belongs the *Kebra Nagast*, which tells the story of the origin of the Ethiopic kingdom and glorifies the newly restored line of Solomon. It was followed by translations of Joseph ben Gorion's *History of the Jews*, of the popular medieval romance known as the *History of Alexander the Great*, and of the *Universal History* of John of Nikiu. This last, which is preserved only in the Ge'ez version, contains historical information of considerable value; its author was an Egyptian bishop who lived not long after the Arab conquest and his is the only trustworthy account of that event which we possess—thanks to the Abyssinians.

In this period the contemporary history of Abyssinia began to be written. For the earlier period we possess only bald lists of kings, so contradictory and confused as to be virtually valueless, and popular romances, generally of a hagiographical character. From the fourteenth century we begin to get more or less contemporary chronicles, compiled from the official annals kept by the king's scribe. The earliest chronicle of any fullness that we possess is

THE RESTORED SOLOMONIAN LINE

that of 'Amda Seyon (Column of Sion) who reigned from 1314 to 1344; it is not contemporary. There is then a gap of nearly a century till the accession of Zar'a Yakob (Seed of Jacob) in 1434. His reign and those of his three successors, Ba'eda Maryam (By the Hand of Mary), Alexander, and Na'od, who died in 1508, were recorded under Na'od's successor, Lebna Dengel (Incense of the Virgin). With the reign of Lebna Dengel begins a series of contemporary chronicles which extend to modern times.

'Amda Seyon has in the chronicle the character popularly attributed to our Henry V. He begins as a profligate and ends as a redoubtable warrior. Early in his reign he seduced not only one of his father's concubines but also two of his own sisters. A monk named Honorius publicly rebuked him and he retorted by flogging Honorius round the streets of the capital. That evening a fire broke out and consumed most of the town and the priests declared that Honorius' blood had turned to flame. The king was sceptical of the miracle, accused the priests of having set fire to the town themselves, and banished them to remote parts of the kingdom. After this he became a new man and began the long series of wars which occupy the remainder of the chronicle. These wars were mostly directed against the series of Moslem kingdoms which had established themselves on the south-eastern borders of the Abyssinian kingdom since the beginning of the second millennium A.D., Ifat, Hadya, Fatigar, Doaro, Bali, and above all Adel, on the Gulf of Aden. There is no need to recapitulate the details of these campaigns, which are wearisome reading. With monotonous regularity the king ravages the Moslem kingdoms, burns their capitals, and receives the submission of their kings. With equally monotonous regularity the Moslem kings ravage the Abyssinian kingdom and annex its border provinces. The Abyssinian armies murmur at their continual hardships in the torrid clime of Somaliland and return home. The king, backed only by a handful of men, performs incredible feats of valour, and his deserting armies return in shame. So the wars go on with very little permanent result. While the Abyssinian armies are in the field some of the Moslem kingdoms temporarily acknowledge the suzerainty of the Abyssinian king and pay him tribute. When they are disbanded they rebel again.

Similar wars occupy a large part of the chronicles of the fifteenth century. By this time most of the minor kingdoms adjoining Abyssinia seem to have been reduced to a more or less regular vassalage. Adel remained the arch-enemy. Apart from these wars there is little to record save during the reign of Zar'a Yakob (1434–68). Zar'a Yakob was not only a great warrior but a great reformer and organizer. He determined to stamp out the remnants of paganism in his kingdom. Every Abyssinian was ordered to wear upon his forehead an amulet inscribed, 'I belong to the Father, the Son, and the Holy Ghost', and on either arm amulets inscribed, 'I deny the devil in Christ the God', and 'I deny Dasek the accursed. I am the servant of Mary, the mother of the Creator of the World.' All who refused were executed and their property confiscated. An army of spies was organized to smell out secret idolaters. The grand inquisitor was one of the chief officials of the kingdom, the Keeper of the Hour, who was served by a staff of servants set apart for the work. These never mixed with the people, having no intercourse with women, and never eating in other men's houses; they might not even cut their hair without the king's permission (the object of this prohibition was presumably to prevent their hair falling into the hands of magicians and being used for casting spells upon them). The unlimited power granted to the Keeper of the Hour caused him to be greatly feared and hated, and eventually the king yielded to the popular tumult and deposed him from his office. Zar'a Yakob's zeal for religion was not merely negative. He ordered that the priests should give public instruction in the faith outside the churches every Sunday, and he moreover published the faith that they were to teach. Under his auspices seven books were issued containing the doctrine, laws, and customs of the Church. The king confirmed the rule that the Sabbath should be observed like Sunday, and that monthly festivals should be held in honour of the Nativity, Our Lady, and other saints, and ordered that in every church there should be an altar to Our Lady. He suppressed the heresy of 'the Sons of Stephen' who would not bow the knee to Our Lady and the Cross. He built and endowed innumerable churches.

Zar'a Yakob did not confine his attention to the Church. He also reorganized the secular administration of the kingdom. On this subject the chronicle is more vague, merely stating that he divided up the provinces anew, instituted a new class of governors, and fixed the tribute.

Under Zar'a Yakob the Abyssinian Church was reconciled with the Roman see. Pope Eugenius IV entered into negotiations with the Coptic patriarch of Alexandria and with Nicodemus, superior of the Abyssinian community at Jerusalem. Zar'a Yakob was informed and authorized Nicodemus to send delegates to Italy with full powers, and these delegates, two monks from the Abyssinian monastery at Jerusalem, together with the abbot of the monastery of St. Anthony, representing the patriarch, attended the Council of Florence in 1441 and signed a decree declaring the submission of the Coptic Church, including that of Ethiopia, to the Roman see. It need hardly be said that the significance of this step was not appreciated in Abyssinia, whose clergy and people had no intention of abandoning the faith of Alexandria and probably had no idea that their representatives had done so. There is no record of these transactions in the Abyssinian chronicles, which only relate that a certain Frank— conceivably a Papal delegate concerned in the negotiations —arrived in Abyssinia in the reign of Zar'a Yakob and, being challenged to a theological disputation, was utterly confounded by the Abyssinian doctors.

This Frank must have been the first western European who penetrated to Abyssinia. In the next reign came another, a Venetian painter named Nicholas Brancaleone. His skill was greatly appreciated and he was commissioned by the king to decorate the walls of many churches with his paintings. One of his pictures, a Virgin and Child, caused a great commotion. According to Western convention he painted the infant Christ on the Virgin's left arm. Now the left arm is in the Near East considered less honourable than the right and the clergy raised a great outcry, declaring that Our Lord was dishonoured and demanding that the picture be destroyed. The king, however, supported the artist and the picture continued to adorn the church for which it was designed till 1709, when it was destroyed in a Galla raid. Brancaleone was never allowed to leave the country and he lived there for more than forty years; in his old age he was met by Alvarez, who describes him as 'a very honourable person and a great gentleman, though a painter'. The numerous paintings which he executed during his long career, many of which were seen by Alvarez in various parts of the country, seem to have had a profound effect on Abyssinian art. The miniatures of the Abyssinian manuscripts, curious and grotesque though they are, show distinct signs of Italian influence in such details as the style of dress.

PART III
i. PRESTER JOHN

DURING the twelfth century western Europe was filled with rumours of a mysterious Christian monarch named Prester John who ruled somewhere in the remote parts of the East. These rumours were crystallized in a letter, published in about 1165, purporting to be addressed to the Emperor Manuel Comnenus by Prester John himself. In this letter Prester John recounts at length the wonders of his kingdom. He ruled over seventy-two tributary kings and his dominions included the three Indias. In them were to be found all the strange beasts recorded in medieval bestiaries, including the salamander which dwelt in fire; from its incombustible envelope were made the Prester's own robes, which were washed not with water but with fire. In his dominions were also the Amazons and the Bragmans and the unclean races of men whom Alexander the Great had walled up in the cities of the north to emerge at the last day. His palace was built according to the designs of St. Thomas, the apostle of the Indies, and contained a marvellous mirror in which he could see all parts of his dominions. He ruled over twenty bishops and twelve archbishops, not to speak of the patriarch of the Indies, the protopope of the Samargantians, and the archprotopope of Susa. Despite this, such was his Christian humility, he took to himself no higher title than that of priest. He went to war preceded by thirteen golden crosses, each followed by ten thousand horsemen and a hundred thousand footmen, and it was his great ambition to march to Jerusalem and annihilate the infidels.

The authenticity of this extraordinary fabrication—though not necessarily the truth of all the statements it contained—was accepted with unquestioning faith in western Europe, and great hopes were entertained of this mighty Christian monarch who would take the Moslems in the rear. The origins of the legend are most obscure. The immediate inspiration of the letter seems to have been a report spread in the Papal court in about 1145 by the bishop of Gabala in Syria. The bishop had heard rumours of a certain John, who was both priest and king, was by religion a Christian though a Nestorian, and reigned in the distant East beyond Armenia and Persia. He had recently, after overthrowing the Medes and Persians, advanced to fight for Jerusalem against the Moslems, but being unable to cross the Tigris had returned to his kingdom. The historical personage who inspired this story seems to have been the Gur Khan, a Turkish prince who had recently inflicted a disastrous defeat on the Seljuk king of Persia. It has been suggested that his title, Gur Khan, may have sounded in Christian ears like Johannes. There is no evidence that he was a Christian, but his defeat of the Seljuk king of Persia is accounted in Moslem historians as one of the greatest blows ever inflicted on Islam and he and his followers are styled Kafirs (infidels). This name was also normally applied to Christians, and the illusion may therefore easily have arisen among Christians who heard the story that the great John who had overthrown the Moslem king of Persia was a Christian. There are, however, clearly other elements in the rumours which the bishop of Gabala picked up. The statement that Prester John was a Nestorian may be due to reports of the Nestorian Christians of St. Thomas in India which had percolated through to the West; there is indeed a circumstantial story that a patriarch of the Indies visited the Papal court early in the twelfth century and told of the wonders of the shrine of St.

Thomas. Rumours may even have reached the West of the Nestorian Mongol tribes which were discovered by European travellers in the thirteenth century and whose khans were identified by them with Prester John.

As the years passed and European travellers explored inner Asia and could find nothing but petty Mongol khans with whom to identify the magnificent vision of Prester John, men began to look for him elsewhere. European travellers in Egypt and Palestine heard rumours of a mighty Christian king who ruled the regions they vaguely described as India or Ethiopia somewhere beyond Egypt, and they concluded that he must be Prester John. The identification of the king of Abyssinia with Prester John was firmly established in the fourteenth century. It is indeed not improbable that rumours current in the Near East about the king of Abyssinia may have contributed to the original legend of Prester John. We know from Abu Salih that the Copts at the beginning of the thirteenth century believed—quite erroneously—that the king of Abyssinia was a priest, and this belief may account for this otherwise inexplicable element in the legend of Prester John. An Abyssinian king may even have been identified with Prester John as far back as 1177, for the king to whom Pope Alexander III wrote in that year and who was fairly certainly a king of Abyssinia is styled by the Pope 'John, the illustrious and magnificent king of the Indians', and is rebuked for his vainglory and boasting, a clear allusion to the famous letter of Prester John to the Emperor Manuel.

The explorers sent out by Prince Henry the Navigator along the African coast to discover an all-sea route from Portugal to the Indies brought back reports of a great Christian king who ruled somewhere far in the interior. These reports tallied remarkably with the then current identification of Prester John as a king who reigned somewhere beyond Egypt, and King John II conceived the idea that the alliance of this mighty Christian king would be very useful in establishing connexion between Portugal and India. He accordingly in 1487 dispatched an expedition under Bartholomew Diaz down the coast of Africa to investigate the possibility of reaching him by sea, and at the same time sent an envoy, one Peter de Covilham, to the Levant to endeavour to establish contact by that route. De Covilham succeeded in entering Abyssinia and reaching the king, but he was never allowed to return; Alvarez met him at the Abyssinian court some thirty years later. Meanwhile Diaz's expedition had not succeeded in rounding the Cape but had established that there was a sea route to India, and ten years later Vasco da Gama rounded the Cape and reached India. Their object achieved, the Portuguese seem for a time to have lost interest in Prester John. But presently they began to realize that he might be a useful ally against the various Moslem principalities of the Gulf of Aden and the Persian Gulf, who seriously hampered their trade by their raids, and in about 1510 Albuquerque, governor of the Indies, landed two envoys at Cape Guardafui; these reached the Abyssinian court, but did not return. Their coming seems, however, to have aroused interest in the Abyssinian court, for a year or two later Matthew, an Armenian, was dispatched by the queen regent, Helena, to India and eventually reached Portugal. The authenticity of his credentials was suspected by the Portuguese and he was coldly received. Eventually, however, it was determined to dispatch a regular embassy to Prester John, and in 1520, in the reign of Lebna Dengel, it was landed at Arkiko, near Massaua, by the governor of the Indies. This embassy stayed six years in Abyssinia but was at length permitted to return, and its chaplain, Francisco

PRESTER JOHN 63

Alvarez, subsequently published an account of it and a description of the country. Alvarez's account is of high value, not only as the first description of Abyssinia by a foreigner, but as the only description of Abyssinia in its medieval glory before its civilization was wrecked by the Moslem and Galla invasions.

ii. THE MEDIEVAL CIVILIZATION OF ABYSSINIA

The official title of the King of Abyssinia was, and still is, Negusa Nagast, or king of kings, of Ethiopia. His grandiloquent title is justified by the fact that he ruled over an agglomeration of petty kingdoms. Some of them were ruled by hereditary kings, tributary vassals of the king of kings. This applied especially to the outlying pagan and Moslem kingdoms to the south and east. The king endeavoured to attach these subordinate royal families to himself by marrying their daughters; the polygamy which this policy involved was to a certain extent atoned for by the conversion of the princesses to Christianity. The policy was by no means always successful. Alvarez states that the wars of Lebna Dengel's reign were caused by his having refused to marry the daughter of the king of Hadya on the ground that she had projecting front teeth; having been converted to Christianity she could not be restored to her Moslem father and was married to one of the Abyssinian nobility, an insult which was deeply resented. The policy also led to the curious result that the daughter of a Moslem king might be regent of Abyssinia; for during a minority the queen-mother ruled. In fact Helena, who first opened negotiations with the Portuguese, was daughter of the Moslem king of Doaro. No evil effects seem to have followed from this; Helena indeed was an excellent ruler.

In the central parts of the kingdom the tributary kingdoms had long been reduced to provinces. They were still called kingdoms. Some of the governors, the Bahrnagas, for instance, or King of the Sea, who ruled the maritime province, were still styled kings. But they ruled at the king's pleasure; during Alvarez's stay four successive governors ruled the maritime province. The same applied to the subordinate governors to whom Alvarez gives the title of ras and shum. They were not allowed to leave their lands save on a summons from the king, and if a summons came they went to court carrying their families and possessions with them, for they did not know if they would return. On arrival at court they encamped on the outskirts and awaited a message from the king. They might wait ignored for several months. In the meanwhile they went about stripped to the waist. On receiving their summons they presented themselves, still stripped to the waist, and having at last learned for what purpose they had been summoned and whether they were to be confirmed in their governments or dismissed, they resumed their normal clothes. According to Alvarez changes were very frequently made and the power of the king was absolute.

Each ras and shum was responsible for the military contingent of his district. When Alvarez was at court he constantly saw them arriving with bodies of troops and being dispatched to the seat of war. The governor was responsible for the tribute of the whole province, each subordinate governor paying his quota to him. Alvarez witnessed the payment of the tribute of the kingdoms of Gojjam, Tigré, and Bahrmedr (the maritime province). The kingdom of Gojjam had belonged to the queenmother Helena and, as she had recently died and no governor had been appointed, one of the Favourites, the principal ministers of the kingdom, collected and delivered

THE MEDIEVAL CIVILIZATION OF ABYSSINIA 65

the tribute. He presented himself stripped to the waist a little way from the king's tent and cried three times, 'Sire!' The reply came, 'Who are you?' He answered, 'I who call am the smallest of your house, I am he who saddles your mules and bridles your baggage mules, I serve you in whatever you command. I bring you, Sire, what you commanded me.' The reply was given, 'Pass on', and he advanced followed by the tribute. First came three thousand horses, then three thousand mules. There followed three thousand men each carrying a heavy cotton cloth, such as were used as blankets, then three thousand men each carrying ten light cotton cloths. At the end came three men each carrying a tray covered with green and red cloths; on them was the gold tribute, which was thirty thousand ouquias. The whole procession took ten days to pass. The tribute of Tigré and Bahrmedr was presented in similar form. It consisted of horses and silks and stuffs. This pageant was no doubt arranged to impress the Portuguese embassy and it produced the desired effect. Alvarez comments indeed on the very poor quality of the horses and mules, but the quantity and richness of the stuffs amazed him. It may be noted that there was no currency in Abyssinia. The tribute was collected in kind. For purposes of trade blocks of salt, and in some districts lumps of iron, were still used as they had been in the days of Cosmas.

The king's revenue greatly exceeded his expenditure. His expenditure was very small. His army consisted of bodies of men at arms provided by the governors, rases, and shums at their own expense. The troops in so far as they did not live on the country brought their own provisions with them when on campaign. The governors of all grades lived on the tribute of certain villages in their governments which were assigned for their maintenance. The great officers of state were similarly maintained by fiefs granted to them by the king. The abuna and the churches and monasteries were supported by other villages and lands; these were held in perpetuity and not like the fiefs of the secular lords at the king's pleasure. All the rest of the land belonged to the king and paid tribute to him. The only regular expense which fell on the king was the maintenance of himself and his immediate entourage. He was of course expected to reward his officers with lavish gifts from time to time. He also sent gifts to neighbouring kings periodically, but in this way he normally got as much as he gave; the only unreciprocated gifts were those sent to the patriarch of Alexandria and the sultan of Egypt, for which the king got nothing in return save a new abuna. The king constantly made lavish donations to the Church, building new monasteries and churches and enriching those that already existed with gold and silks and stuffs. But a large surplus remained which was hoarded in pits and caves scattered about the country or in impregnable ambas. Peter de Covilham assured Alvarez that in one of these caches, which was near his own house, there was enough gold to buy the world; every year he had seen a large quantity put in and he never saw any taken out.

The exact extent of the territory ruled by the Abyssinian king at this date is rather difficult to determine from Alvarez's account. Bahrmedr stretched according to him to the neighbourhood of Suakim—he is not clear whether it included this town or not. On its way to seek the king the embassy passed through the kingdoms of Tigré, Amhara, Angot, and Shoa. Later Alvarez paid a visit to the court when it was in the kingdom of Fatigar, and passed an Easter on the borders of Goragé, which was an unsubdued pagan district. Alvarez never visited the western half of the Abyssinian dominions and he is rather vague about these regions. He heard of the important kingdoms of Begamedr and Gojjam and Damot, the last only partly converted to Christianity, and beyond Damot he heard vague stories of Gafat, a pagan country still apparently unsubdued. He does not mention the rich kingdom of Dambya around Lake Tsana, but he heard of the existence of Christian Nubians north-west of Abyssinia. The Christianity of Nubia was at this time in its final agony. During the stay of the Portuguese embassy the Nubians sent an embassy to the king of Abyssinia begging him to send them priests; for they had lost touch with Egypt, whence they got their bishops. The king in a rather uncharitable spirit refused, saying that he got his abuna from Egypt, how then could he give priests since another gave them to him? It was about this time that the Moslem kingdom of Sennar was established on the north-west frontier of Abyssinia.

The kingdom had at this time no fixed capital. The king still went to the ancient capital, Axum, to be crowned, but he spent his life marching round his kingdom and his moving camp was his capital. The camp was as large as a town and it was laid out on a regular plan. A large level plain was chosen and on its highest point were pitched the five tents that housed the king himself. These were surrounded by a wall of curtains, or, if the camp were more permanent, a stockade pierced by twelve gates. In front, that is to the west, was an open space flanked by two churches, St. Mary and the Holy Cross, each with two other tents attached to it, in one of which the bread for communion was baked and in the other the vestments and furniture were stored. Beyond these churches lay two large tents in which the king's treasures were kept. North of the king's enclosure was the camp of the pages, south that of the queen. Behind, to the east, were the two kitchen tents with a church attached to them. Directly facing the royal enclosure to the west, a long way off (Alvarez says two crossbow shots), was a long tent which served as a court of justice and adjacent to it two tents for the two Chief Justices, two more for prisons, and another which was the church of justice. Proceeding west again, there was another large open space in which were chained the four lions which accompanied the king wherever he went. Beyond them again, at such a distance that it could not be seen from the king's enclosure, was the church of the market. On either side of the king's camp were the camps of the two Favourites, of the Abuna, of the Keeper of the Hour, and of the other high officers, and beyond them the tents of the nobility. Flanking the market encamped the merchants, bakers, smiths, and the rest of the common people.

The camp moved in a similar set order. The king did not always accompany it, preferring to travel in less state and stop at monasteries by the wayside. When he moved in state he rode on a mule led by six pages within a moving enclosure of red curtains held up on poles. In front marched twenty pages, headed by six saddled mules and six saddled horses, each led by four men. With him always went the four lions led each by two chains, and a hundred men each carrying a jar of meat and a hundred men each carrying a basket of bread. The portable altars of the churches were also carried in great state on trestles covered with precious cloths. Each altar was carried by four priests with four other priests in attendance and was preceded by two deacons, one with thurible and cross, the other with a bell to warn people off the road.

The king normally lived in sacred seclusion within his enclosure, seen only by his pages and the high officers of state. He displayed himself to his people on a high platform three times a year, on Christmas Day, Easter, and

Holy Cross Day. This was a recent innovation in Alvarez's day, introduced because King Alexander's death had been concealed by the courtiers for three years, during which they had disposed of the kingdom at their pleasure. The officers of the king's household were theoretically hereditary in the great families which claimed descent from the Israelite nobles sent with Menelik by King Solomon. These offices had now apparently become sinecures and their titular holders were very numerous, since every son succeeded to his father's office. Actually the nobility was excluded from service about the king's person, since it had been found that too many state secrets leaked out. The kings, either inspired by their Moslem neighbours or following the same train of reasoning, employed as their pages Moslem or pagan boys captured in war whom they educated as Christians. Those of them who proved capable and trustworthy were admitted to the select body which served the king's person. The king thus possessed a body of servants devoted to his service, who had grown up in it and had no other ties. The great officers of state were nominated by the king. The two chief ministers, who were also the commanders-in-chief, were the two Favourites, of the right hand and the left. There were also two Chief Justices, of the right hand and the left. Other important officers were the king's secretary and the Keeper of the Hour, his chaplain.

Justice was very rough and ready but strongly centralized. Attached to every provincial governor and every ras was a judge and an official described by Alvarez as a notary, both appointed directly by the king. The judge tried in the first instance and in minor cases his decision was final. Major cases he referred to the governor. There was an appeal from the governor to the Crown in certain circumstances, and the notary certified the cases in which an appeal should be allowed. The procedure in the court of the royal camp is thus described by Alvarez. In the tent of Justice were set up thirteen chairs, a tall chair in the centre and six small on either side. No one sat on these chairs, which were merely symbolic. The judges sat on the ground, divided into two groups, of the left and of the right, for everything was thus divided. The plaintiff and the defendant were then produced and each made a speech and each a reply before the judges to whose jurisdiction they belonged. Then a man whom Alvarez describes as the doorkeeper summed up and gave his judgement. Each of the judges then followed suit, and finally the Chief Justice summed up all the arguments and gave the final decision. If any question of fact was at issue the court was adjourned till this question could be settled. Important cases were judged before the Favourites and the Judges of Appeal, standing in the open space before the king's enclosure; they acted only as mouthpieces for the king, reporting the arguments of the litigants to him and returning with the questions which he asked and finally with his judgement. Nothing was committed to writing; the whole procedure was entirely oral. It is probable that the law administered was customary, for the only written code of Abyssinia, the *Fetha Nagast* or Judgement of Kings, was a collection of canon law, drawn up in the twelfth century by a Copt and later translated into Ge'ez. Such a code, compiled from the canons of ancient ecclesiastical councils, was obviously quite unsuited for the government of a kingdom like Abyssinia.

Prisoners awaiting trial were kept chained in the two prison tents adjoining the tent of Justice. They were expected to provide not only for their own maintenance but also for that of their guards, unless they had been arrested on the demand of a private person. In that case

THE MEDIEVAL CIVILIZATION OF ABYSSINIA

their accuser had to feed them and their guards and they could claim to be released if food was not provided. Punishments were manifold and some of them barbarous; mutilation of various kinds was common. Political offenders of high degree were often relegated to ambas situated in remote parts of the kingdom. The commonest penalty for venial offences was flogging. This often looked more brutal than it was. The prisoner was stripped to the waist and staked to the ground. Four executioners then beat him with heavy whips that could cut to the bone. Normally, however, they struck the ground by the prisoner, only actually striking him two or three times, or even not at all, according to instructions received. Alvarez saw the Chief Justices flogged several times for alleged miscarriage of justice, but they were none the worse after, nor any less respected.

One of the most extraordinary customs of the kingdom was the seclusion of all the male line of the royal house save the reigning king and his sons and grandsons. Descent was strictly in the male line and the king's daughters and their descendants, having no claim to the Crown or indeed to any honour, were allowed to live freely where they wished. But as each king was crowned all his brothers were relegated to an impregnable amba and there they lived and died with their families, completely cut off from all communication with the kingdom. They were amply provided with revenues and the king often bestowed rich gifts upon them. But they were strictly imprisoned by a select body of guards and none might enter the amba under the most frightful penalties. When Alvarez was at court a monk smuggled out a message from one of them; it was rumoured that it was an appeal to the Portuguese to release them. The message was intercepted and the monk and the guards who had failed in their trust were arrested

72 THE MEDIEVAL CIVILIZATION OF ABYSSINIA

and flogged for days continuously. Women of the royal line were allowed to leave the amba, and it is not clear how strictly the more distant collateral lines were secluded; they seem to have lived in the same mountainous region but not in the actual fortress. The nearer kinsmen of the king were never released except when the direct royal line failed and one of them was summoned to the throne. The origin of the custom is shrouded in antiquity. According to the story told to Alvarez it was instituted by the mythical Abraha, the first Christian king. In Abyssinian tradition the pagan queen who wasted the kingdom in the tenth century captured Debra Damo, then the mountain of the princes, and slew all the line of Solomon save one boy, from whom was descended Yekuno Amlak (Let him be king), the restorer of the Solomonian line. The custom, abandoned after this frightful disaster, is said to have been revived either by a son or grandson of Yekuno Amlak, in about 1300, or by Ba'eda Maryam (1468–78), who selected another amba, Amba Geshen, for the purpose. Shortly after Alvarez's stay Amba Geshen was sacked by the Moslem invaders and its occupants massacred. The custom then lapsed again but was revived by Basilides (1632–65), who chose Amba Wahni for the purpose. The custom still survived when Bruce was in Abyssinia (1768–73), but seems to have lapsed in the subsequent civil wars.

Being a priest Alvarez was much interested in the Abyssinian Church and devotes many pages to describing its ceremonies and customs. His account makes very pleasant reading, for he does not, like most subsequent writers, either carp or jeer at the peculiarities of Abyssinian Christianity. His sympathetic attitude is partly due to his date. He was a medieval Catholic and did not suffer from the narrow-minded self-righteousness which was produced by the Reformation and the Counter-Reformation. His own Church, moreover, was still at a stage of culture not very far removed from that of Abyssinia. But some credit must also be given to his personal character. He was a man of remarkable breadth of mind. He frankly condemned such practices as he considered definitely uncanonical, and he was not afraid to declare his views openly to the abuna or to the king himself. But customs which were merely strange he viewed with tolerance. He was rather shocked at the barbaric yelling and dancing by which the liturgy was accompanied on great occasions, but he admitted that, since they were intended for the glory of God, they were good. He also recorded dispassionately what Catholic customs shocked the Abyssinians; they had for instance, he observed, a curious objection to the habit of spitting in church.

Alvarez was greatly impressed with the multitude of churches and monasteries, which were apparently more numerous even than those of medieval Europe. Wherever one went there were five or six churches in view and every high hill was crowned by a monastery. He admired many of the buildings. In the greater churches the sanctuary was substantially built of stone, divided by stone pillars and arches into aisles and vaulted; the walls were covered with paintings. The sanctuary, which was square, was surrounded by one or more circular enclosures, sometimes of stone, sometimes of wood, and the whole was covered with a thatch roof; these enclosures were also either painted or hung with rich stuffs.

This is still the regular church plan to this day. Romantic persons have seen in the circular form an imitation of the Jewish temple. There is, however, no evidence that the Abyssinians shared the delusion of the Templars that the Dome of the Rock was Solomon's temple, and the fact that the cathedral of Axum, which, as housing the Ark of the Covenant, should imitate the temple most closely, is and always has been rectangular in plan, seems to indicate that the circular plan has no symbolic significance. It is in fact the normal indigenous plan of all buildings, churches and houses alike, and is dictated by the form of the roof; corners are difficult to make in thatch. How old it is cannot be said, since so few old churches have survived in Abyssinia and those that survive have never been scientifically examined. The primitive churches were certainly of the normal basilican type, and in the thirteenth century the churches of Lalibala were still rectangular in plan; but these were certainly of foreign inspiration.

Alvarez was also impressed by the vast number of monks and priests, which was so great that the endowments of the churches and monasteries, huge though they were, were unable to support them. This applied particularly to the royal churches, which were served by an order of priests whom Alvarez calls canons. This order, which was supposed to be descended from Azarias the son of Zadok, was strictly hereditary, every son of a canon becoming a canon. The result was that the staff of every royal church eventually became by natural increase too numerous for its endowments to support, and the canons were reduced to great poverty. In order to relieve them the kings continually founded new royal churches and drafted off the superfluous canons of the old churches to them. Alvarez disapproved of the way in which the clergy, including the monks, pursued secular avocations and in particular engaged in trade; only the old monks lived in the monasteries and the young all earned their living outside. On the other hand, he was edified by the austere life which the older monks lived in the monasteries and was greatly impressed by their self-mortifications during fasts; a common practice was to sit all night up to the neck in a tank of icy water. He also speaks highly of the morality of the secular clergy, whose family life contrasted very favourably with that of the laity; the average priest was faithful to the one wife which canon law allowed and indeed enjoined upon him, and if on her death he did remarry he was deprived.

Of the ceremonies which Alvarez witnessed, that which shocked him most was the ritual bathing at Epiphany. One feature of the ceremony which shocked him was that the bathers, both men and women, were stark naked. The other point was doctrinal. He had got into his head that the rite was baptism and he was horrified that baptism should, contrary to the fundamental law of the Church, be repeated. He seems to have got at crossquestions with the interpreter, for when, on being asked his opinion of the rite, he expressed this objection, the answer was given that many turned Moslem or Jew and on returning to the faith had to be rebaptized. The answer is quite beside the point, for the Epiphany bathing, though a commemoration of our Lord's baptism, is not baptism, and the whole population, headed by the king, and the abuna, who had certainly not apostatized, took part in it. Alvarez also witnessed the consecration of priests and deacons by the abuna. Ordinations took place nearly every day, and the abuna was continually escorted by large crowds shouting, 'My lord, make us priests and deacons. And may God grant you a long life.' One day two thousand three hundred and fifty-seven candidates presented themselves for the priesthood. They were marshalled on a wide plain and the abuna rode out on his mule and made a proclamation in Arabic which was translated into Abyssinian. It was to the effect that any one who had or had had more than one wife must depart under pain of excommunication. The candidates then advanced in three queues to three priests who made them read a few words out of a book after which they were stamped with a seal in ink on the right arm. They then filed past the abuna, who laid his hands on their heads and recited a few words over them. The abuna then said Mass and all the new priests communicated. The only point which shocked Alvarez in this ceremony was that the candidates were inadequately clad and that some of them were, contrary to canon law, blind or maimed. The abuna promised to rectify these errors. The ordinations of deacons was similar, save that there was no examination in reading. The candidates were all unmarried, mostly boys and some babes in arms. Alvarez objected to the ordination of infants, but the abuna replied that he was now very old and there was no knowing when another abuna would be obtained—there had been an interregnum of twenty-three years before his own arrival—and therefore provision must be made for the future. Alvarez subsequently became quite intimate with the abuna. When first he came to the country (according to his own account fifty years ago, but his chronology is contradictory and confused) he had been a zealous reformer and had persuaded the then king to forbid the keeping of the Sabbath and the avoidance of pork and unclean meat. But the native clergy had won the day, for they pointed out that Brancaleone and de Covilham (who had gone native) observed the Mosaic law and argued that it must be the universal law of the Church if even Franks observed it.

iii. THE PORTUGUESE EMBASSY

The reception given to the Portuguese embassy was on the whole very friendly. The king, when he had convinced himself that they were Christians, displayed a deep interest in their religious faith and practice. He had long interviews with Alvarez, repeatedly made him vest himself and explain the liturgical significance of each vestment, watched the celebration of the Mass with great attention and apparent pleasure, made him produce all the holy books he had with him and had passages translated; he was greatly interested in the *Flos Sanctorum* and asked many questions about the western saints of whom he had never heard. Alvarez was also subjected to frequent theological catechisms. In these he floundered unhappily, for he was no theologian and his knowledge of early church history was shadowy in the extreme. Luckily neither party seems to have realized the doctrinal chasm which separated them and the question of the nature or natures of Christ was never raised. Alvarez always tried to bring the argument round to the one point of which he was certain, the supremacy of the Roman see. He produced all the stock arguments and these, being in the true style of Abyssinian theological disputation, seem to have created an impression. The king seems to have been greatly attracted and impressed by the Catholic Faith, as expounded by the tactful Alvarez, and was more anxious to bring the customs of the native Church into conformity with those of the Roman Church than was Alvarez himself. The abuna was also very friendly. Of the attitude of the native clergy not much is said, but they were apparently more suspicious. It was they, probably, who inspired the catechisms on such awkward points as the celibacy of the clergy, which was, they alleged, contrary to the canons of Nicaea; Alvarez, however, knew nothing about the Council of Nicaea except that it was held under the presidency of Pope Leo and formulated the Nicene Creed —neither of which assertions is true.

The final upshot of the religious discussion was that the king entrusted to Alvarez a letter to the Pope, declaring his submission to the Holy See. On the political side the negotiations did not run so smoothly. The king was dissatisfied with the rather meagre presents which the embassy brought and the hectoring tone of the ambassador cannot have created a good impression, especially since he quarrelled openly with the members of his staff. A hitch, moreover, occurred when the Portuguese showed the king a map. On this map the dominions of Prester John occupied in the medieval manner a vast space—even after the return of the embassy the ideas of the Portuguese on the extent of Abyssinia remained grossly exaggerated, and it was hoped to open more convenient communications with the country via the Congo or 'some other river which flows to the Cape of Good Hope'. The kingdoms of Europe were, on the other hand, marked very small, and the king's faith in the power of Portugal was evidently shaken. He suggested that the kings of France and Spain and Portugal should co-operate in the contemplated crusade against the Moslem neighbours of Abyssinia. This was naturally not at all to the mind of the Portuguese. When the king realized that the Christian kings of Frankland were not at peace with one another he expressed his deep sorrow; if he had a Christian neighbour he would love him as a brother. However, an agreement was eventually reached. The Captain-General of the Indies had suggested that the king should cede Massaua as a naval base to the Portuguese. To this the king willingly consented, and also suggested the seizure of Zeila; Suakim was also mentioned. The king promised his assistance with men, food, and money. In return he asked for artificers of all kinds, masons, carpenters, goldsmiths, armourers, and also doctors. He also asked for lead that

Prester John's Kingdom, from Ortelius (1570)

he might roof his churches more permanently than with thatch.

Lebna Dengel's letter to Manuel of Portugal is, as the first extant diplomatic communication of an Abyssinian king, worth quoting. The Abyssinians took the art of epistolography very seriously and marvelled at the casual way in which the Portuguese wrote down what they wanted to say without any reference to books. The king and his learned men laboured for days, surrounded by piles of holy books. The letter was written in Abyssinian, Arabic, and Portuguese (the Portuguese version was produced by de Covilham aided by Alvarez and the clerk of the Portuguese embassy), and all these versions were copied in duplicate and each of the two sets of letters was enclosed in a little bag of brocade. The result of their labours was the following: the translation is from the Portuguese copy.

'In the name of God the Father, as always was, in whom we find no beginning. In the name of the Son, one only, who is like him without being seen; light of the Stars, from the first before the foundations of the ocean sea were founded: who in former times was conceived in the womb of the Virgin without seed of man or making of marriage: so was the knowledge of his office. In the name of the Paraclete, spirit of holiness, who knows all secrets, where he was first in the heights of heaven, which is sustained without props or supports, and extended the earth, without its being from the beginning, nor was it known nor created from the east to the west, and from the north to the south; neither is the first nor the second, but the Trinity joined together in one Creator of all things, for ever by one sole counsel and one word for ever and ever. Amen.

'This writing and embassage is sent by the Incense of the Virgin, for that is his name by baptism, and when he became king he was named King David,[1] the head of his kingdoms,

[1] It may be noted that every king of Abyssinia takes a new name

beloved of God, prop of the faith, a relation of the lineage of Judah, son of David, son of Solomon, son of the Column of Sion, son of the Seed of Jacob, son of the Hand of Mary, son of Nahum in the flesh;[1] emperor of the high Ethiopia and of great kingdoms, lordships and lands, King of Xoa, of Cafate, of Fatiguar, of Angote, of Barua, of Baliganje, of Adea, and of Vangue, King of Gojame, of Amara, of Bagamidri, of Dambea and of Vague, and of Tigrimahom and of Sabaim, where was the Queen Saba, and of Barnagais, lord as far as Egypt.[2] This letter goes to the very powerful and most excellent king Don Manuel, who always conquers, and who lives in the love of God, and firm in the Catholic faith, son of Peter and Paul, King of Portugal and the Algarves, a friend of the Christians, an enemy of the Moors and Gentiles; Lord of Africa and Guinea, and of the mountains and islands of the moon, and of the Red Sea, and of Arabia, Persia and Ormuz, and of the great Indies, and of all its towns and islands; Judge and Conqueror of the Moors and strong Pagans, lord of the Moors and very high lands. Peace be with you king Manuel, strong in the faith, assisted by our Lord Jesus Christ to kill the Moors, and without lance or buckler you drive and cast them out like dogs. Peace be with your wife, the friend of Jesus Christ, the servant of our Lady the Virgin mother of the Saviour of the world. Peace be with your sons at this hour, as to the flowers and fresh lily at your table. Peace to your daughters, who are provided with clothes like good palaces. Peace be with your relations, seed of the saints, as the Scripture says, the sons of the saints are blessed and great in grace in their house. Peace to those of your council and offices and to the lords of your jurisdiction. Peace to your great captains of the camps and frontiers of strong places. Peace to all your people and

on ascending the throne, and as he is called by his throne name or his baptismal name indifferently, confusion often arises.

[1] These are translations of the names of Lebna Dengel's ancestors, *vide supra.*, p. 55.

[2] Many of these names are misspelt. Tigrimahom and Barnagais are the Portuguese versions of the titles of the governors of Tigré and the maritime province, which the Portuguese took to be local names.

populations who are in Christ. Peace to your great cities and to all those that are within them that are not Jews or Moors, only to those who are Christians. Peace to all the parishes which are in Christ and to your faithful grandees. Amen.'

The main body of the letter is correspondingly verbose and need not be quoted in full. The king recapitulates the history of the various embassies from that of Matthew onwards. He records his joy on seeing the crosses carried by the Portuguese envoys and thus learning that they were Christians. He recounts the miracles which guided them on their way to Ethiopia. He recalls an ancient prophecy in the *Life and Passion of St. Victor*, that a Frank king should meet a king of Ethiopia and they should give each other peace. He boasts of his victories over the 'Pagans and Moors, dirty sons of Mahomed, and others are slaves who do not know God, and others pay reverence to sticks and to fire and others to the sun and others to serpents'. He urges Manuel not to rest till he has taken the holy house of Jerusalem. He then returns to the embassy and praises its members, especially Alvarez, 'a just man and very truthful in speech'. The practical part of the letter, the concession and requests, occupies less than a tenth of the whole.

iv. THE MOSLEM INVASIONS AND THE PORTUGUESE EXPEDITION

Storm clouds had recently been gathering on the horizon. In 1516 the Ottoman Sultan Selim had conquered Egypt and received the submission of the Hejjaz. The advent of the Ottoman power created a profound change in the political situation on the Red Sea. It infused new life into the dormant spirit of the jihad, the sacred war of Islam against the infidels. It moreover supplied new weapons to the Moslem princes with which to conduct this war. The Turks introduced firearms into this area and, what was as important, supplied to the local princes disciplined bodies of troops capable of using firearms.

Both the Abyssinians and the Portuguese were vaguely aware of the danger. The Abyssinian king was interested in the few matchlocks which the Portuguese had brought with them and included gunsmiths in the craftsmen which he asked of the Captain-General of the Indies; they occupy, however, a curiously subordinate position in his letter. The Portuguese wished to forestall the Turks in occupying naval bases on the Red Sea, and the Abyssinian king heartily supported them. Neither party, however, realized the urgency of the danger. The Abyssinian king dallied six years with the embassy and the Portuguese, when the embassy returned, failed to act for many years. Meanwhile, the king of Adel had been watching the negotiations between the two infidel powers with close attention and he struck promptly.

The very next year after the Portuguese embassy had sailed from Massaua the attack began. The leader of the armies of Adel was Ahmed ibn Ibrahim el Ghazi, surnamed Gran, or the left-handed, a general of very remarkable ability. He realized the immense importance of the new weapons and he obtained from the Turks by gifts or tribute a small corps of matchlockmen; it normally numbered about two hundred. The effect produced by this tiny body of disciplined regulars, skilled in the use of firearms, was catastrophic. The Abyssinian armies broke and fled like chaff before the wind. The whole of Abyssinia was overrun and Ahmed proceeded systematically to reduce the Abyssinian strongholds. The treasure fortresses were captured and the accumulated wealth of the kingdom was carried off. The churches and monasteries were looted and burnt. Amba Geshen itself was taken and the princes of the Solomonian line put to the sword. In the words of the Abyssinian chronicles nine men out of ten renounced the Christian faith and turned Moslem. Only the king with a scanty band of faithful followers maintained the struggle, eluding his pursuers in the mountain fastnesses of the interior.

In his distress Lebna Dengel naturally thought of the Portuguese, and in about 1535 he succeeded in smuggling out of his kingdom one John Bermudez, a humble member of the Portuguese embassy whom he had detained as a hostage for his own ambassador. Bermudez succeeded eventually in reaching Portugal and the Portuguese king decided to send a relieving force from India. Communication with Abyssinia had in the meanwhile grown much more difficult. While the Portuguese remained inactive the Turks had in 1538 occupied Yemen and established strong garrisons in all the seaboard towns, including Aden, and a powerful Ottoman fleet now controlled the Red Sea. In 1541, however, the Portuguese, in the course of a raid on Suez, landed a force of four hundred men at Massaua under the command of Christopher da Gama, a son of the famous Vasco.

Lebna Dengel had died the previous year and his son Claudius was now king. Claudius was at the moment far away in the south, in Shoa. The Portuguese were, however, received by Isaac, the Bahrnagas, and the Queen-Mother, who was living in a neighbouring fortress. The party reached Debaroa, the capital of Bahrmedr, and there it stopped for the rains. In December it began to move southwards in order to effect a junction with the king. Ahmed, who was near Lake Tsana, was determined to prevent this junction and he attacked the Portuguese force. He possessed an overwhelming superiority in numbers, but on the other hand the Portuguese had twice as many matchlocks as he. Two battles were fought, neither of which was conclusive. The Portuguese, though severely handled, maintained themselves. On the other hand, Ahmed succeeded in delaying their progress till the rains set in again. He thereupon retreated eastwards to the plain of Danakil. He saw that if he was to crush the Portuguese what he wanted was more Turks. He accordingly sent gifts, including Minas, King Claudius' brother, whom he had captured in 1539, to the pasha of Zabid, a Turkish garrison town on the opposite coast of Yemen, and asked for reinforcements. The pasha sent him nine hundred matchlockmen, and Ahmed promptly attacked the Portuguese camp. His victory was complete. More than half the Portuguese, including Christopher da Gama their general, were killed, and their camp with their arms and ammunition taken. After this victory Ahmed thought that he could neglect the scattered remnants of the Portuguese force, and dismissing the Turks except for his regular force of two hundred, he returned to his head-quarters near Lake Tsana.

Ahmed's confidence was, however, premature. Shortly before his defeat and death, Christopher da Gama had by a daring attack seized a wellnigh impregnable amba which commanded the route to the south. The Queen-Mother and the surviving Portuguese sought refuge on this amba, and there they were presently joined by Claudius with his handful of followers. The Abyssinians began to rally to their king, and soon a force of eight thousand foot and five hundred horse was collected. Meanwhile, the Portuguese rearmed themselves from a depot which Christopher da Gama had prudently established near Debaroa, and their chemist, who had luckily escaped, made gunpowder from the sulphur and saltpetre that abounded locally. The Portuguese were burning to avenge their leader, and on their urgent request Claudius marched against Ahmed, who was calmly encamped by Lake Tsana quite unaware of the resurrection of his foe. In the battle which followed Ahmed ventured too close to the Portuguese and he was shot down. Dismayed at the loss of their leader, the Somali troops broke and fled. The Turks fought on stubbornly but were eventually overwhelmed; only forty of the two hundred escaped.

The tide now turned. Deprived of their redoubtable leader Ahmed Gran, the Moslems were no longer formidable. Moreover, Claudius now possessed a small body of disciplined troops, skilled in the use of firearms, such as had been the chief factor in Ahmed's success. For the king of Portugal ordered the surviving Portuguese, who numbered about a hundred, to remain in the country and serve its king; this they did and their descendants gradually mixed with the rest of the population. Claudius rapidly reconquered his kingdom, establishing his authority even in the frontier provinces of Bali, Doaro, and Fatigar. He fought several wars with the pagan Gallas who had already begun to overrun southern Abyssinia. He endeavoured to revive the arts of peace. He rebuilt many churches that the Moslems had destroyed and made fresh copies of the books they had burnt. His otherwise prosperous reign was marred by only one disaster. Towards the end of his reign that which his father had feared and urged the Portuguese to prevent came to pass. The Turks occupied Massaua and stationed in it a strong garrison under a pasha. Henceforth no more military assistance could be hoped for from overseas.

Under Claudius began the religious dissensions between the Abyssinian and Roman churches. Their opening chapter is most unedifying. That John Bermudez who, it may be remembered, had been detained by King Lebna Dengel and had been sent by him to Portugal to solicit aid, returned to Abyssinia with Christopher da Gama's party. As soon as Claudius arrived he announced to him that he was patriarch of Abyssinia and demanded his submission to his authority and that of the Pope. His story was as follows. When the abuna Mark was on the point of death, King Lebna Dengel had ordered him to institute Bermudez, 'in accordance with his custom', as his successor. This the abuna had done, having first ordained him in all the sacred orders. Bermudez had accepted on condition that his appointment was confirmed by the Pope and the king had agreed. Bermudez had then on his way to Portugal visited the Pope and had been confirmed in his office and moreover created Patriarch of Alexandria. The whole story appears to be a tissue of lies. The first part is difficult to test, but it is *a priori* remotely improbable that the abuna would have consecrated him—it was certainly not 'in accordance with his custom'. We possess, moreover, a letter from Lebna Dengel to Bermudez, written on the latter's return from Portugal to India, and the king appears to be quite unaware of Bermudez's supposed ecclesiastical rank. The latter part of the story can be tested. Not only is there no record in the Papal archives of Bermudez's appointment, but at the very date when Bermudez is supposed to have visited the Pope another patriarch of Alexandria is recorded, and while Bermudez was still alive the Pope appointed another patriarch of Abyssinia without alluding to Bermudez's existence. Moreover, Claudius, who was highly suspicious of Bermudez's claims, wrote to the king of Portugal to verify them. We possess the Portuguese king's reply, and in it he states that as far as he knows Bermudez is a mere clerk, but urges that to avoid scandal Claudius should deal gently with him until he, the king of Portugal, can send a genuine patriarch to Abyssinia.

Impostor though he was, Bermudez managed to make himself a great nuisance. Claudius at first refused to acknowledge Bermudez's authority, but finding that he was supported by the Portuguese and being at the moment entirely dependent on their support—this was before Ahmed Gran's death—he presently submitted. After the defeat of Ahmed Gran, Bermudez began to press his claims, demanding that the Roman rite should be enforced throughout the country and that all the clergy should be reordained by him. When the king refused these preposterous demands Bermudez again stirred up the Portuguese against him. There was actually a battle between the royal forces and the Portuguese, but the king thought it more prudent to proceed by guile, and after a pretended submission scattered the Portuguese by granting them estates in different provinces, relegating Bermudez to a remote district. He in the meanwhile secured an abuna from Cairo. Bermudez presently escaped from his place of exile, but the king could now afford to take a strong line and dispatched him with his Portuguese supporters to garrison the frontier province of Doaro. They were shortly expelled by a Galla raid, and after this Bermudez seems to have retired into obscurity; the facts were no doubt by this time becoming generally known. He slipped out of Abyssinia on the arrival of a genuine Papal mission, and returning to Portugal lived in modest retirement for many years. Long after he published a narrative of his career in which he set forth all his old pretensions and, such is the power of impudence, his claims were until comparatively recently believed by many historians.

v. THE JESUIT MISSION—OVIEDO

The newly founded Society of Jesus was deeply interested in the reports brought back of Abyssinia. Ignatius Loyola himself desired to spread the true faith among its people. This was forbidden by the Pope, but when King John III of Portugal suggested the dispatch of a Latin patriarch to Abyssinia, the Pope determined to entrust the mission to the Jesuits, and on the suggestion of Loyola John Nunez Barreto was consecrated patriarch with Andrew de Oviedo and Melchior Carneiro as bishops to assist and eventually succeed him. The king of Portugal dispatched them to India, ordering his viceroy to install them with a force of five hundred men at their back. The viceroy was unable to spare such a force, and as he had by a preliminary mission discovered that Claudius would by no means welcome the arrival of a patriarch from Rome, he decided not to risk the person of the patriarch—who in fact died some years later in India, never having seen his province—but to send Oviedo with a few priests. Oviedo landed at Arkiko in 1557, just before the Turks occupied Massaua in force and closed further communications.

Bermudez's antics cannot have predisposed Claudius in favour of the Roman Church. They had revealed what the Roman supremacy really meant. It is difficult to see what precisely Lebna Dengel had intended by his submission to the Pope. He probably merely wished to acknowledge his rank as the first bishop in Christendom —a position which all the Eastern Churches would allow to him if he were not a heretic. It is highly unlikely that he envisaged receiving an abuna from him instead of from the patriarch of Alexandria; he says nothing of it in his letter to the Pope. He certainly would not have expected his abuna, by whomsoever appointed, to challenge the royal power. The king had always been supreme in Abyssinia in all causes, as well ecclesiastical as civil. The abuna might advise the king, but he could not give orders. Bermudez had tried to do this, and when resisted had not hesitated to raise a rebellion.

Claudius might well then have disliked the prospect of another Roman patriarch, even if he had, like Lebna Dengel, been attracted by the Roman faith. But in fact he was a zealous adherent of the national faith. He was also far better informed than his father in theology and was well aware that the Franks were Nestorians and believed in four gods. When therefore the Jesuit mission arrived he not only refused to admit Oviedo's authority, stating that he had an abuna from Alexandria already, but he affirmed his belief in the orthodox faith of Alexandria. At the same time he declared himself open to conviction. The Jesuits fell into the trap. Bermudez, who was a completely uneducated man, had avoided theological discussions and insisted simply on his authority, and his blustering and bullying had caused grave disorders in the kingdom. The Jesuits, who were learned men, were betrayed into long theological disputes. The abuna and the native clergy could not stand up against them, but the king, as they freely admit in their own dispatches, often drove Oviedo into a corner. We possess a Confession of Faith written by Claudius himself in answer to Oviedo. The first half consists of a clear exposition of the monophysite position. The second half is a defence of the peculiar customs of the Abyssinian Church. Claudius wisely if somewhat disingenuously minimizes the importance of these. The sabbath, he says, we do not keep as the Jews keep it, but we celebrate it by offering up the sacrament. Circumcision is only a custom of the people, like the scarification of the face in Ethiopia and Nubia, and the slitting of the ears in India. As for the distinction of clean and unclean meat, every man is free to abstain from the flesh of animals; some love to eat fish, some love to eat the flesh of cocks, some abstain from the flesh of lambs; let every man follow his own desire. Claudius seems to have enjoyed these discussions and was highly indignant when the abuna threatened to excommunicate him for reading a dissertation of the errors of the Abyssinians which the Jesuits had translated into Ge'ez. He treated the Jesuits with uniform kindness and respect, and they speak very highly of his character, saying that but for his obduracy he would have been a perfect king.

Claudius was killed invading Adel (1559). He was succeeded by his brother Minas, the same who had been captured by Ahmed Gran and given by him to the pasha of Zabid. He had been ransomed by Claudius, but his captivity seems to have soured his character. He was a man of violent temper and a bigoted adherent of the national Church. Claudius had allowed the Abyssinian wives and slaves of the Portuguese to adopt the Roman faith, and had permitted the Abyssinians to attend the Roman churches. Minas forbade this, and when Bishop Oviedo defied him was barely restrained from killing him with his own hands. The bishop was several times banished to mountain fortresses and several times threatened with death, but bravely stood his ground. In the meanwhile the ferocity of Minas had caused Isaac, the Bahrnagas, who knew that the king had a grudge against him, to rebel. He was supported by the captain of the Portuguese, and this fact naturally threw suspicion on Oviedo, who was further ill-treated. Minas defeated Isaac, and Isaac in desperation allied himself with Samur, the pasha of Massaua, ceding to him most of his territory, including his capital Debaroa. The subsequent events are differently told in different sources. Another battle followed, and according to one account Minas was victorious but immediately withdrew to Shoa; according to another he was defeated. At all events, when he died shortly afterwards (1563), the Jesuits were in Isaac's camp, either having sought refuge there of their own accord or—this is their own account—having been captured after Minas' defeat.

Minas' son, Sarsa Dengel, had a long and successful reign (1563-97). It was occupied almost entirely with wars. He suppressed the rebellion of the Bahrnagas and defeated the Turks and the king of Adel who came to his assistance. He fought with the Falashas of Semien. He was chiefly occupied, however, in the south, where he waged innumerable campaigns against the Gallas. He penetrated farther south than any Abyssinian king is recorded to have done before; to him is due the conversion of the Negro-Hamitic peoples of Enarya and Kaffa to Christianity. In religion he followed the national faith but he allowed the Jesuit mission to preach in peace. The mission settled down at Fremona, near Axum, and there the patriarch Oviedo—he had succeeded to the title on the death of Barreto in 1562—died in 1577. It is difficult to judge of his character. He has been accused of fomenting rebellion under Minas, and the charge, though not proved, is not improbable, for it is on record that he repeatedly tried to send letters to the king of Portugal urging him to send five or six hundred men to subdue the kingdom. For this, however, he can hardly be blamed, for Minas' intolerance was in his eyes the greatest obstacle to the propagation of the faith, and he thought that if the fear of punishment was removed the Abyssinians would flock to the true Church. During the tolerant reign of Sarsa Dengel he does not seem to have caused any trouble, although his authority was not acknowledged. He was undoubtedly a learned theologian and a brave man, and in his later years he won the deep respect of his Abyssinian neighbours by his holy and austere life. But he seems to have lacked tact and persuasiveness and he was a very unsuccessful missionary.

vi. THE JESUIT MISSION—PAEZ

The Jesuits at Fremona gradually died off and the mission was finally deprived of all its priests. The members of the Society in India were anxious to relieve it, but the difficulties were almost insuperable, since the Turks at Massaua kept a careful watch and prevented any priest from entering the country. In 1595 a Maronite priest, who it was hoped might as an Arab not be suspected, was dispatched, but he was betrayed. The next year Melchior de Sylva, a native Indian Christian, had better fortune. In 1603 he was followed by Peter Paez, a Spaniard. He had tried to reach Abyssinia before but had been detected and held captive in Yemen for seven years. He did not despair, however. He settled at Diu, a Portuguese factory in India, representing himself to be an Armenian. Here he established friendly relations with a Turk, the aga of the pasha of Suakim, who paid frequent visits to Diu for trade. Paez represented to him that he wanted to return to his native country, but was afraid of being enslaved by the Turks on the way. The aga immediately promised to see him safely to Jerusalem. Paez then casually inquired if they could stop on the way at Massaua, as he wished to collect the property of some friends who had died in Abyssinia. The aga said that it would be quite convenient and that he would arrange for the journey up-country. Paez's scheme was successfully carried out and he duly arrived at Fremona.

Paez had the advantage over Oviedo that he was not burdened with the rank of patriarch or bishop. He was thus not obliged to stand on his dignity or claim authority. But, what was more important, he was personally a complete contrast to Oviedo. He was clearly a man of great personal charm and was able to adapt himself to any company in which he found himself; the intimate friendship he struck up with a Turkish janissary is proof enough of this. He was a man of the most diverse accomplishments. He was a brilliant linguist and rapidly acquired a thorough knowledge not only of Amharic but of Ge'ez. He was an able schoolmaster, and he later trained himself to be an expert architect, mason, and carpenter. But above all he was a man of great patience and discretion; he never tried to move too fast. These qualities he showed from the first. He did not, like the other missionaries, present himself at once at court. He settled down quietly at Fremona, proceeded to learn the languages and presently opened a school for the Portuguese and such Abyssinians as chose to entrust their children to him. The school soon became very popular as the Abyssinian nobility found their sons acquiring a knowledge of the Ge'ez language far superior to that of the native clergy. Paez subtly began his propaganda by teaching his pupils a Catholic catechism which he had translated into Ge'ez.

Since the death of Sarsa Dengel there had been a disputed succession and civil wars. Sarsa Dengel had wished his nephew Za Dengel to succeed. The Queen-Mother, backed by a few powerful nobles, who preferred minority rule, put one of Sarsa Dengel's sons, a boy named Jacob, on the throne. Confused intrigues and wars followed. Eventually, not long after Paez's establishment at Fremona, Za Dengel won the day. One of the Portuguese officers mentioned the good work that Paez was doing in Tigré and the king summoned him to court. He presented himself with two of his star pupils, a theological discussion followed in which the two boys confounded the Abyssinian clergy, and Paez delivered a sermon in Geʻez which took the audience by storm by its eloquence and purity of diction. The king was greatly impressed and soon privately informed Paez of his conversion. Unfortunately the zeal of the royal convert outran the bounds of prudence, and despite Paez's protests he immediately began to issue decrees forbidding the observance of the Sabbath and abolishing all the errors of the Abyssinian Church. The king's position was none too secure, a fact which he clearly realized, for at the same time that he wrote to the Pope to render his obedience he wrote to Philip III of Spain (and Portugal) asking the hand of his daughter for his son and the loan of troops, professedly against the Gallas. The nobles who were of the opposing party did not delay to strike. They raised a rebellion and induced the abuna to take a step unprecedented in Abyssinian history, to release the Abyssinians from their oath of allegiance to the king. Za Dengel's army melted away and he was defeated and killed.

Another period of confused intrigues and fighting followed, and eventually in 1607 Sisinnius, another nephew of Sarsa Dengel, was acknowledged king. Sisinnius, who relied on the support of the Portuguese, protected Paez and kept him at court. He was at once attracted by Paez's personality and seems to have been soon converted to the Catholic faith. Early in his reign he wrote to the Pope and also to the king of Spain, renewing his predecessor's request for troops. But he did not fall into Za Dengel's mistake. He spent the first five years of his reign consolidating his position, re-establishing the royal power over the governors, suppressing pretenders, and reducing the Agaus, the Falashas, and the Gallas to obedience. In 1612 the king's brother, Se'ela Kristos,[1] who was governor of Gojjam, was converted and helped the Jesuits to establish a mission in his province. Shortly afterwards the king proclaimed that the doctrine of the two natures of Christ was true. The abuna excommunicated him, but Sisinnius compelled him to retract the excommunication. A plot was then formed to assassinate the king. It was foiled in rather a curious way. Paez had built for the king a palace on the shores of Lake Tsana. It was a very remarkable feat. Paez himself was not only architect but personally trained the workmen and worked with his own hands. The palace was the wonder of the Abyssinians, for it was, as they expressed it, a house upon a house, that is, it had two stories. At the top of the grand staircase was a small room and Paez had fitted its door with a spring lock, saying that it might be useful one day. It now proved its usefulness, for the king, suspecting the conspirators' purpose, but not being certain of their guilt, led them upstairs, and entering this room slammed the door in their faces. They promptly proved their guilt by fleeing and raising a rebellion which was crushed. The king then forbade the observance of the Sabbath. Another rebellion followed, which was again crushed. About this time the king made further efforts to enlist the interest of the Pope and the king of Spain and, fearing that letters sent via Massaua might be intercepted by the Turks, he sent his emissaries, two Jesuits, southwards in the hope that they might reach the coast at Malindi (north of Mombasa). The two fathers penetrated as far as the upper waters of the Omo, but were forced eventually to retrace their steps. Their account of the strange customs of the barbarous peoples through which they passed is extant and makes curious reading.

[1] Ras Se'ela Kristos is the original of Johnson's Rasselas.

Finally in 1622 the king made a solemn profession of the Catholic faith and issued a long proclamation in which he expounded the true doctrine of Chalcedon and exposed the vices of the recent abunas, who had all apparently been men of the loosest morals. Unhappily at this moment Paez died, and the king was deprived of a faithful servant, an inspiring teacher, and a prudent adviser.

vii. THE JESUIT MISSION—MENDEZ

Paez's successor was a man of a very different stamp. Sisinnius asked the Pope to send him a patriarch, and the Pope, encouraged by Paez's reports, complied. His choice fell on Alphonzo Mendez, like Paez a Spanish Jesuit, but otherwise unlike him in every way, overbearing, narrow-minded, and bigoted. Mendez and his staff succeeded in landing in the kingdom of Danakil, which, though Moslem, was at this time more or less subject to the king of Abyssinia. The king of Danakil, in obedience to his suzerain's orders, conveyed Mendez to the Abyssinian frontier where he was received with great state and conducted to the king. Mendez's first act was typical of the man. He ordered that a solemn assembly of notables be held, and in their presence Sisinnius had to kneel and swear fealty to the patriarch as representative of the Pope. This ceremony was not calculated to enhance the prestige of the Crown. Mendez then proceeded to reform the Church. The Jesuits had naturally detected many irregularities. With ruthless logic the patriarch set them right. Doubts had been raised as to the validity of the abuna's orders and the form of ordination he used was so brief as to be hardly canonical. The patriarch accordingly suspended all priests till they could be reordained by him. It was alleged that the words used in baptism were sometimes invalid. So all the population was to be rebaptized. Circumcision was forbidden. The churches were reconsecrated and altars of the Roman form erected and graven images, such as the Abyssinians considered idolatrous, introduced. The calendar was brought into conformity with that of Rome. The liturgy was remodelled, though on the request of the king it was permitted to be celebrated in Ge'ez. Everything was done in fact that could antagonize not only the clergy but the simple worshipper. The Jesuit historians themselves admit that Mendez's zeal was sometimes carried to excess. A greatly revered abbot of the famous monastery of Debra Libanos had been buried in the church. When Mendez heard this he declared that the church was defiled by the body of a schismatic, and the corpse was dug up and thrown out with the utmost disrespect. Another incident that aroused great feeling was the arrest of a woman for witchcraft. For the Abyssinians, as the Jesuit historian explains with disapproval, do not, despite the clear evidence of the scriptures, believe in witchcraft.

The reforms, as might be expected, met with stubborn resistance which was answered by violent measures. Revolt after revolt broke out, and these revolts were not merely the work of discontented and ambitious nobles but genuine popular insurrections. Sisinnius succeeded in suppressing them one by one, but the kingdom fell into disorder and the Gallas took the opportunity of increasing the confusion. As the civil wars went on without any prospect of ending, the king's loyal followers, including his own son Basilides, began to urge him to retract and his army began to murmur against the continual wars in which they won neither glory nor booty and subdued not pagans or Moslems but their own fellow Christians. The king himself, though still firmly convinced of the truth of the Catholic faith, thought it wise to compromise, but when he tried to do so Mendez upbraided him severely for his presumption. But at last, in 1632, having subdued a peculiarly obstinate insurrection with great carnage, Sisinnius could endure it no longer and he issued the following proclamation: 'Hear ye! Hear ye! We first gave you this faith believing that it was good. But innumerable people have been slain, Julius, Gabriel, Takla Giorgis, Sarsa Kristos, and now these peasants. For which reason we restore to you the faith of your forefathers. Let the former clergy return to the churches, let them put in their altars, let them say their own liturgy. And do ye rejoice.' After this pathetic confession of failure he abdicated in favour of his son Basilides, and soon afterwards died in the faith for which he had fought so long.

Basilides had been consistently loyal to his father while he reigned despite many attempts to seduce him from his allegiance. This had not been due to any affection for the Roman faith, and as soon as he held the reins of government he completely reversed his father's religious policy. Sisinnius had intended, even after his final renunciation, to allow toleration to the Roman religion, thus returning to the situation which had existed under Claudius, Sarsa Dengel, and in the earlier part of his own reign. Basilides saw that religious feeling had been too much exacerbated for a compromise to be possible, and when Mendez, suddenly cast down from his power, proposed various concessions, he sternly replied that he was resolved to extirpate the Catholic faith, and would soon deport the Jesuits; in the meanwhile they were to be concentrated and interned at Fremona, and all arms and ammunition in their possession were to be surrendered. Not only was Basilides afraid of continued civil war if Catholicism was still preached—for a number of Abyssinian notables had with the late king adopted the faith with fervour, and there were still the remnants of the Portuguese to be reckoned with—but he was in terror of armed intervention on behalf of the Jesuits from abroad. In this he was to certain extent justified, for the Jesuits, when they reached India, strongly recommended the governor-general to send four hundred men to occupy Suakim and Massaua as a base for the conquest of Abyssinia.

The Jesuits were determined, if possible, to remain in the country and continue their missionary efforts. Several succeeded in finding refuge with friendly Abyssinian nobles. Mendez, with the main body, eluded their guards and fled to the Bahrnagas, John Akay, who was in rebellion. He received them kindly at first, but on being threatened with punishment if he kept them, and promised full pardon if he surrendered them, he gave way. He declared that he could not surrender them to the king, since this would be a breach of the laws of hospitality, but he reconciled it with his conscience to sell them to the pasha of Suakim. The pasha treated them comparatively well and resold them to the Spanish government at a very considerable profit. Basilides then hunted down the remaining Jesuits that lurked in the country; these he executed summarily, since they had defied his authority. He likewise banished and confiscated the property of all Abyssinians who still clung to the Roman faith; a few highly placed recusants, including Se'ela Kristos, his uncle, he executed.

When the news of the apostasy of Abyssinia reached Rome, the Congregation of the Propaganda, divining that the disaster might have been partly due to the uncompromising character of the Spanish Jesuits entrusted with the mission, determined to make another attempt with priests of a different nationality and order. Accordingly, six French Capuchins were dispatched. Two tried to enter Abyssinia via Magadocha; they were killed by the natives before reaching Abyssinia. Two succeeded in entering the country via Massaua; directly they were detected they were stoned. The remaining two turned back from Massaua on hearing the fate of their comrades. The result of this mission was that Basilides, determined to be pestered no more, made an agreement with the pashas of Suakim and Massaua that they should execute all priests who tried to land. This treaty bore fruit in 1648 when three other Capuchins landed at Massaua. They had been foolish enough to announce their coming to Basilides. He notified the pasha, who promptly beheaded them and, flaying their heads, sent the skins to Basilides, that he might know by their colour and tonsure that the Frankish priests had been faithfully killed.

Thus ended a lamentable chapter in the history of the Church. The Jesuits certainly had a difficult task. The Abyssinians had from centuries of isolation developed a strongly conservative and nationalist spirit. In particular they were deeply attached to the doctrines and customs of their ancient national church. Their reception of the first representatives of Western Christianity who visited them was, it is true, on the whole friendly, and the king at any rate had seemed willing to admit that abuses existed and was anxious to reform them. It must remain doubtful, however, how far the clergy and the general mass of the people would have followed the king. The Jesuits did not make the best use of their opportunities. One cardinal error was the sending of Latin patriarchs to the country. If this did not lead to a clash with the king it made the new faith highly unpopular with his subjects, who regarded it in the light of a foreign domination. It would no doubt have been necessary to break the connexion with Alexandria, but it would have been more politic to induce the kings to found a national church under the general suzerainty of Rome. A second error was the controversy on the doctrinal question. This was inevitable at that date, though in more modern times the Roman Church has seen the wisdom of allowing the uniate churches to preserve such variations in their creeds as the omission of the Filioque. The third error was the interference with local customs like circumcision. This was unenlightened even according to the standards of the time, and Paez seems to have disapproved of it. Mendez carried this third error to a fantastic extreme and capped all by treating the Abyssinians, a proud Christian people who had defended and propagated their faith for centuries against a surrounding infidel world, as if they were pagans, rebaptizing them, reordaining their priests, and reconsecrating their churches. If the Jesuits had contented themselves like Paez with a policy of education and had, like him, restrained instead of spurring on the fervour of their royal converts, it is conceivable that they might have succeeded. As it was they so embittered the national suspicion of the Abyssinians towards foreigners that the Christian king of Abyssinia employed his hereditary enemy, the Moslem Turk, to keep Christians out of the country. The hatred and suspicion of Catholics sank deep into the heart of the people, and a century and a half later the Scottish traveller Bruce was deeply suspect till he explained that his church was even more bitterly opposed to the Pope than the Abyssinian Church could possibly be.

viii. ABYSSINIA IN THE SEVENTEENTH CENTURY

The Jesuits brought back much information about Abyssinia as it was in their day, and this information was drawn up into a book by Balthazar Tellez, a Portuguese Jesuit, shortly after the expulsion. His general tone is one of disillusionment. The golden vision of Prester John had faded to a drab reality and he saw in Abyssinia a poor and undeveloped country and its people as backward and barbarous. Even Alvarez's account he found too glowing and accuses him of being a dupe and a romancer. In this he was unjust. He did not realize, on the one hand, that his own standards were far higher than those of Alvarez, for European culture had progressed enormously in the century that had passed between the arrival of Alvarez and the departure of the Jesuits. On the other hand, he forgot that in the interval Abyssinia had undergone a terrible disaster, the invasions of Ahmed Gran and of the Gallas, that its ancient wealth had been pillaged and its ancient buildings destroyed, and that orderly government and the arts of peace had received an enormous setback. Tellez's tone may be gathered from the following passage:[1]

'We will here give an Account of the Meanness of that Prince's Table, to compare it with the Grandeur of the Ancient *Romans*. Two Tables were plac'd in the Antichamber, a small one for the Emperor and a larger for the Fathers, both of them without any curious Damask Cloth, or Napkins, or gilt Plate. When Dinner Time came, a Curtain was drawn betwixt the Emperor's Table, and that for the Fathers, an inviolable Custom in *Ethiopia*, where no Man sees the Emperor at Dinner, but only two or three Servants that Wait. Then came in ten Women, bringing the Dinner, they in the same Dress as those who serve Great Ladies, being a Sort of Gown of course Cotton Cloth, very long and wide, girt about with a great Sash, over which the Gown being drawn up hangs in large Folds. These Women bring two or three *Macobos*, which are like large Table baskets, and very lofty, because cover'd with high Lids, like Caps, the whole made of Straw or Rushes of several Colours. In these *Macobos*, or Baskets, were 20, or 30 *Apas*, that is thin Cakes, like our frying Oat Cakes, made of Wheat, Pease, and their Grain call'd *Tef*. These *Apas* are very large, and thin, at least half a yard Diameter, and some three

[1] Translation of John Stevens (1714).

Quarters. After these Women follow'd others, bringing several Sorts of Pottage, or Broth, in black Earthen Porringers, covered with Things like Hats, made of fine Straw, the Body of these Hats being very tall, and slender, but the Brims broad, to cover the Porringers, which are also very wide but not deep. The Table is a round Board, an Ell, or yard and a half Diameter, plac'd on Carpets on the Ground, which they cover all over with the *Apas*, without any other Cloth, or Napkins, and on those *Apas* they place the Porringers. And this is all the State of the *Ethiopian* Tables, for they have neither Knife, Fork, nor Spoon, Salt, Pepper Caster or any other Utensil. And it is to be observ'd, that those very *Apas* which serve instead of Napkins, and Dishes, are also part of the Food. When the *Barindo*, which is the raw Beef, being the greatest Dainty at the Table, is brought in, they lay it on the *Apas*, and the Emperor of *Ethiopia* himself takes out a little Knife he carries about him, and cuts the Beef, or has it cut by Pages, who only wait at Table, without any Steward, Controler, Carvers, Cup-bearers, or any other Officers. The same Pages put the Morsels into his Mouth, which Custom is observ'd, not only by the Emperors, but by all the Great Men of *Ethiopia*, who look upon it as too much Trouble to feed themselves. Nor is this the worst, for these Morsels are generally of the soft of the Bread, or of the *Apas* crumbled in the Hand, wetted in several Liquors and so Moulded over, as if they were kneading it, and sometimes these Morsels are so big, that they scarce can be put into the Mouth, and yet they thrust them in, much as we cram Chickens. Thus much as to the Emperor's Table. And indeed those Emperors are much in the right, in not suffering any Body to see such a disagreable way of Feeding.'

Tellez has reliable information on the extent of the Abyssinian kingdom. On the north it still stretched some way beyond Massaua inland, though the coast belonged to the Turks. On the east the kingdom of Danakil, though not tributary, was within its sphere of influence. Its extent to the south is very difficult to define, for most of the country south of the Blue Nile was overrun by the Gallas; Damot, north of the river, was also in their power. Shoa, though it suffered severely from their raids, was thoroughly Abyssinian. Kambate, around the Lake of Shala, was subject to the king of Abyssinia. The mountainous provinces of Enarya and Kaffa were inhabited by Christian peoples, the former of whom, at any rate, paid tribute to the Abyssinian king. Elsewhere the king's writ did not run. A vivid picture of conditions in the south is given by the emissaries of Sisinnius who traversed these regions in 1614. Directly they crossed the Blue Nile they were in enemy territory. Convoyed by a party of Gallas in the pay of the king they marched for several days through a desolate country infested by roving tribes till they reached Enarya. Here they were in civilization once more. They wished to go on south again to Kaffa, but were obliged by the governor of Enarya to turn east. They passed through another desolate area in constant terror of the Gallas till, crossing the Omo, they reached the pagan kingdom of Gingiro, the last that feared the name of the emperor of Ethiopia. The king was occupied in making magic when they arrived, but after a week he received them, standing on top of a high wooden tower on which he dispatched all public business. On being presented with Sisinnius' letter he climbed down the staircase at the back to receive it, in order to show his respect. The envoys tell of the many curious customs that prevailed in Gingiro. If the sun presumed to rise before the king, the latter stayed indoors all day and could perform no business. If the king was wounded or sickened he was immediately dispatched by his subjects. The succession to the throne was a most curious and barbarous proceeding. The king being dead all the men of the royal family scattered and hid themselves in the undergrowth. Then a body of electors went forth and, guided by a great bird, tracked down the future king. On being discovered he resisted furiously, but being overpowered was escorted home. The fighting was not yet over. One noble family had the right of assaulting the electors, and if they could wrest the king from them they enjoyed the honour of enthroning him. The funeral of the old king then took place. His corpse, wrapped in the hide of a newly slaughtered cow, was dragged round the country with the object of fertilizing it, and finally placed in a pit into which was poured the blood of innumerable cows, slaughtered on the spot for several consecutive days. Meanwhile the king's house and property were burned and his favourites and servants all slaughtered to bear him company.

Tellez has much to say of the Gallas. They were a roving people and lived on their herds, not cultivating the ground. For these reasons they were particularly difficult to subdue, since on being attacked they moved off with their herds, leaving a barren country behind them in which the invading army starved. They were great horsemen and their raiding parties moved with great rapidity, looting and destroying everything they passed. They were an intolerable nuisance to the kingdom, but never a serious danger, for they had no cohesion; groups of tribes periodically united for a raid under a common chief, but their union lasted no longer than the campaign. They were quite as willing to fight for the king of Abyssinia as against him, and the king had settled a large body in Dambya province near Lake Tsana; these formed an important part of the royal army. The Gallas did one great service to Abyssinia. They so weakened the once mighty kingdom of Adel that it ceased to be a danger.

Tellez is very contemptuous about the revenue of the Abyssinian kings. Only two provinces paid gold tribute,

Gojjam and Enarya, and the tribute from the latter was very difficult to convey to the king and was often captured by the Gallas. For the rest the tribute was, as in Alvarez's day, in stuffs and horses; the central provinces of Dambya, Gojjam, and Begamedr provided grain also. The Galla raids had involved the loss of much tribute and also remissions; Gojjam, for instance, was excused its tribute of horses that its people might be better able to defend themselves. To make up for these losses the kings had instituted new taxes, one cow out of ten every three years, and one piece of cloth for every loom. There were also internal customs stations at various points, but the revenue from them was mostly granted to the local lords.

The two Favourites had been abolished. Instead there was one prime minister, commander-in-chief and viceroy of the kingdom, styled the ras or head. In the troubled times that followed Ahmed Gran's invasions, much of the ceremony which surrounded the king had been dropped. He now no longer rode surrounded with a moving enclosure of curtains; he was veiled from sight only on formal occasions and during his meals. Tellez gives an interesting account of the ritual of the coronation at Axum. The king, preceded by his army and the officers of state, marched to the cathedral. Outside it his way was barred by a cord held across the road by a number of noble maidens. The maidens asked him, 'Who are you?' He replied, 'I am King of Israel', but the maidens refused to let him pass saying, 'Then you are not our king'. The king made a second attempt with the same result. The third time he answered, 'I am King of Sion', and cut the cord with his sword, the maidens replying, 'You are truly our King of Sion'. Then followed thunderous applause, volleys of gun-fire, blowing of trumpets, and beating of kettledrums. The king was then received by the abuna and clergy and was crowned in the court in front of the cathedral. The crown is described by Tellez as 'a Hat with broad Brims, lin'd with blue Velvet, and cover'd with Gold and Silver Plates, shap'd like Flower de Luces, and some false Jewels'. The king bore no sceptre but a sword. The proceedings ended with Mass in the cathedral, at which the king communicated.

PART IV

i. THE PERIOD OF ISOLATION

BASILIDES, as might be expected, is not represented in a favourable light by the Jesuit historians. They accuse him of slaughtering his twenty-four brothers and of apostatizing to Islam; they add that in his reign the kingdom was overwhelmed by the Gallas and consumed by swarms of locusts. On the last two counts the impartial historian can hardly hold Basilides to blame even if they were true. The Abyssinian chronicles do not in fact record more than the usual quota of Galla wars, and it may be doubted whether the locusts really did flourish more abundantly in Basilides' reign even though the Jesuits were no longer there to exorcize them. Basilides certainly did not become a Moslem, though in fear of the menace of a European invasion he did court the Moslem powers. He certainly did not massacre all his brothers. On the contrary, he revived the old custom of segregating the members of the royal family on an amba, Amba Wahni. He was no doubt a stern ruler, but a stern ruler was needed in order to re-establish the kingdom after the continual civil wars of the last reign. In this Basilides was successful. During his long reign (1632–65) he fought many wars, but he finally reasserted the royal power and was able to devote himself to peaceful works. He built at Gondar, north of Lake Tsana, a new capital which remained until the middle of last century the royal residence. Nor did he neglect the old capital Axum, where he rebuilt the cathedral which had been in a ruinous condition ever since the devastation of Ahmed Gran.

He was succeeded by his son John, whose fifteen years' reign was mainly peaceful. In this reign renewed efforts were made by Catholic missionaries to penetrate Abyssinia.

A party of Franciscans smuggled themselves into the country, but were soon detected and promptly stoned. A little later an admirable opportunity was offered. One of the king's sons suffered from a skin disease, and it was reported to him that there was a Capuchin in Cairo who could save him. The Capuchin was summoned and three Franciscans determined to accompany him. Unfortunately they were impatient of the Capuchin's dilatoriness and started without him. When they appeared at court, and it was revealed that the doctor was not among them, they were immediately stoned. From these facts it is evident that John was as hostile to Franks as his father had been. He seems to have been something of a bigot. He collected and burned all the Catholic books which survived from the Jesuit period. He was intolerant also to the Moslems, whom he compelled to live in separate quarters in the towns. He himself took a great interest in theological disputes. The controversies with the Jesuits seem to have stimulated theological speculation among the Abyssinian clergy. Faced by the arguments for the Chalcedonian faith they felt the need for defining their own position more exactly, and in so doing they disagreed among themselves. Disputes had begun under Sisinnius; they continued under Basilides, and came to a head under John. The points at issue are, to a Western mind, extremely subtle. The chief controversy raged about the Unction of the Holy Spirit which Christ is said to have received on his baptism. On the Chalcedonian view of the two natures the explanation is simple: it was the human nature which was anointed. On the monophysite view difficulties arise. One view, held by the monks of the order of Takla Haymanot, led by those of the great monastery of Debra Libanos, was that the Unction was the grace of the Holy Spirit given to Jesus Christ in his humanity at the moment of the Union of the two natures and that its effect was to restore the dignity of humanity which had been lost by the fall of Adam. The chief opposing view was that supported by the monks of the order of Eustathius. They held that the Unction effected the Union of the two natures. There were various other schools of thought of less importance. One curiously resembles the early heresy of aphthartodocetism. Its adherents held that Christ's body was not a normal human body but was composed of special divine and immortal substance. These controversies long continued to rage. Towards the end of the eighteenth century a new view began to find favour, that of the Three Births. They are the eternal generation by the Father, the birth from the Virgin Mary, and the Unction by the Holy Spirit. Frequent synods have decided that one or other of these views or variations of them are orthodox; in Bruce's day each king was expected to hold a synod on his own accession and also on the arrival of each new abuna. The questions at issue have, however, never been finally settled and the three principal schools of thought, that of the order of Takla Haymanot, that of the Eustathians, and that of the Three Births, still flourish in the Abyssinian Church.

John was succeeded by his son Jesus. He reigned for twenty-four years (1680–1704) and seems to have deserved the style of the Great which was accorded to him. He was, as all good Abyssinian kings have to be, a great warrior, but he was not bloodthirsty. In addition to his wars the chronicles record something rare in Abyssinian history, an administrative reform. Jesus checked the rapacity of the collectors of customs, establishing uniform rates throughout the kingdom. Another of his notable deeds was his visit to the princes on Amba Wahni. The exiled princes always tended to be neglected and to be cheated of the revenues assigned to them by the peculations of their guards. Jesus went personally to hear their complaints and restored their revenues. He re-established the authority of the crown over the Church which his father's excessive religiosity had impaired; he plainly stated that the king only could hold a synod, and that he was not going to hold synods except when he pleased, which was rarely. Finally he relaxed the rigidly anti-European policy of his two predecessors. In his reign fell two attempts to establish diplomatic relations between the court of Abyssinia and that of France. One had a comic conclusion, the other a tragic. Neither had any result whatsoever, but their story is worth telling.

Their expulsion from Abyssinia and the subsequent preference of other orders for missionary work in Abyssinia by the Pope had long rankled in the mind of the Jesuits. The Jesuit advisers of Louis XIV conceived a scheme for recovering their lost prestige. They represented to the king that an embassy from the emperor of Ethiopia would add *éclat* to his court, and the title of Converter of Ethiopia would be a fitting addition to that of Most Christian King. Their scheme was that an envoy should be sent to Abyssinia to represent to its king the advantages of an alliance with the greatest power of Europe, and in particular to induce him to send an embassy to Versailles bringing with it a number of noble Abyssinian youths and maidens to be educated at the French court. Accordingly, Monsieur de Maillet, the French consul in Cairo, was instructed to seek out a suitable envoy and to find ways and means of conveying him to the Abyssinian court. As it chanced an opportunity offered itself at once. An agent of King Jesus, one Hajj Ali, happened to be in Cairo, and he was again looking for a doctor, for Jesus still suffered from a skin complaint. Now in the French community in Cairo there was a druggist, one Poncet. De Maillet got into touch with Hajj Ali and represented to him that Poncet was a famed physician (and he was indeed quite competent to treat Jesus' complaint). It was arranged that Hajj Ali should escort Poncet to Gondar, Poncet was provided by de Maillet with letters in Arabic, stating the ulterior objects of his mission, and a Jesuit, named Brevedent, accompanied him disguised as his servant. The party travelled safely to Abyssinia via Sennaar. Shortly after their arrival in Abyssinia Brevedent unfortunately died of dysentery, but Poncet went on, was presented at Gondar, and successfully treated the king. The story now becomes rather obscure, for we have only Poncet's narrative to rely upon, and he did not know the language of the country. It is improbable that Jesus took the embassy very seriously, since it brought no gifts, essential in oriental diplomacy. It is remotely improbable that he would have consented to send the noble youths and maidens required without escort through the Ottoman Empire, where they were certain to be enslaved. However, he was gratified by his cure and he determined to send an envoy in return. The envoy selected was one of the agents he employed to do his business abroad, a Moslem Armenian named Murad, whose qualification for European diplomacy was that he had once been cook to a French merchant in Aleppo. Murad was provided with letters in Arabic expressing the king's gratitude and with some gifts, stuffs, some Abyssinian slaves, and a young elephant. Poncet and Murad then started for Cairo by sea. Here their misfortunes began. The elephant died; Murad providently cut off its ears as a proof that it had been sent. When they landed at Jidda the Sharif of Mecca seized three of the slaves. The stuffs were lost in a storm on the Red Sea. On their arrival at Cairo Poncet put on airs as envoy plenipotentiary to the court of Ethiopia. This infuriated de Maillet, an irascible old Norman noble. He demanded to see the letters from the Abyssinian king. Poncet haughtily replied that they were for the eyes of the king of France only. Foiled in his curiosity, de Maillet induced the pasha of Egypt to impound the letters. The Jesuits, hearing of this and unaware of de Maillet's part in the story, raised a storm at the gross breach of diplomatic privilege. The Sublime Porte, alarmed at the prospect of a breach with France, sent a commission to investigate the affair. The pasha revealed the truth and the Porte ordered de Maillet to pay the expenses of the commission, which by Ottoman law fell on the guilty party. De Maillet's hatred of Poncet was redoubled by this scandal, and he did everything in his power to discredit him, even representing that he was a complete impostor and had never been to Abyssinia. Undeterred, Poncet and Murad proceeded on their journey; on leaving Cairo the authorities confiscated their last Abyssinian slave. Eventually they arrived at Versailles and the ambassador of the king of France, Monsieur Poncet, the Cairo druggist, introduced the ambassador of the emperor of Ethiopia, Murad, the Armenian ex-cook, who presented the gifts of the emperor of Ethiopia, the decaying ears of an elephant.

De Maillet had done his work well. The unfortunate Poncet was regarded with the deepest suspicion. He had written an account of his journey which though ignorant and somewhat pretentious—he was an uneducated man— has been vindicated by Bruce as an honest account of what he saw and was told. This account was subjected to savage criticism by the savants of France, who, taking up de Maillet's insinuations, satisfactorily proved that it was a romance. They objected that Murad was not an Ethiopic name—which is not surprising, seeing that its bearer was a Moslem Armenian. They pointed with scorn to the description of Gondar; such a town did not even exist, it was nowhere mentioned in the Jesuit accounts. This, again, is not surprising since it was built after the expulsion of the Jesuits. Poncet spoke of there being many towns in Abyssinia. It was well known that there was only one town in Abyssinia, Axum, and the people lived in tents. Poor Poncet was completely discredited by these revelations and returned a disappointed man to his pharmacy in Cairo.

The French government was not discouraged by this fiasco. It was decided that another ambassador of more trustworthy character and higher social standing should be sent, and it was suggested to Monsieur de Maillet that he himself, since he knew the Levant so well and had so successfully unmasked the impostor Poncet, would be a suitable person. De Maillet, however, had no intention of exchanging the comforts of Cairo for a laborious journey through savage lands, and, excusing himself on the grounds of ill health, suggested Monsieur du Roule, French vice-consul at Damietta. Du Roule was a young man of ambition and some ability, but was completely ignorant of the manners and customs of the countries he was to visit and had all the Gallic contempt for anything that was not French. He was, in fact, not the man to ingratiate himself with the African kings through whose territory he was to pass. His journey was dogged from the start by mysterious intrigues in which Bruce's venomously Protestant mind sees the hand of the Franciscan and Capuchin orders. They were, no doubt, jealous of the Jesuits' attempt to poach on their preserves, but it is hard to believe that they went as far as Bruce suggests. There is no doubt that both the Moslems and the Copts were suspicious of the threatened rapprochement between France and Abyssinia, and it is probably to them that du Roule's misfortunes are to be attributed. He was everywhere treated with discourtesy, he was frequently delayed, he was compelled to pay large sums for permits to proceed. In spite of all this he succeeded in reaching Sennaar. The king received him kindly and his wives showed great curiosity in the white-skinned stranger. Du Roule, thinking to please them, displayed the presents he was taking to the Abyssinian court. He had made a singularly silly choice of presents; the principal item was a set of distorting mirrors. The negro ladies seeing their grotesque reflections fled in terror, crying that du Roule was a magician. Du Roule found himself viewed with suspicion. He tried to leave several times but was turned back. Eventually he and his party were murdered in the open street. Bruce attributes this outrage also to the machinations of the local Franciscan missionaries, who had withdrawn from the town during du Roule's visit.

Du Roule had sent his interpreter, one Elias, an Armenian, ahead from Sennaar to ask Jesus for his assistance. Jesus had sent him back with letters to du Roule and to the pasha of Egypt and the king of Sennaar, asking them to forward du Roule on his way. But before Elias had gone very far he heard that Jesus had been assassinated by one of his sons, Takla Haymanot, who now reigned in his stead. He returned to have his instructions approved by the new king. Takla Haymanot read the letters and ordered them to be recopied in his name. As a specimen of the epistolary style of the Abyssinian kings at this date one of these letters may be cited (Bruce's translation):

'To the Pacha and the Lords of the Militia of Cairo, on the part of the king of Abyssinia, the king Tecla Haimanout, son of the king of the church of Abyssinia.

'On the part of the august king, the powerful arbiter of nations, shadow of God upon earth, guide of kings who profess the religion of the Messiah, the most powerful of all Christian kings, he who maintains order between Mahometans and Christians, protector of the confines of Alexandria, observer of the commandments of the gospel, heir from father to son of a most powerful kingdom, descended of the family of David and Solomon. May the blessing of Israel be upon our prophet and upon them! May his happiness be durable and his greatness lasting! And may his powerful army be always feared! To the most powerful lord, elevated by his dignity, venerable by his merits, distinguished by his strength and riches among all Mahometans, the refuge of all those that reverence him, who by his prudence governs and directs the armies of the noble empire and commands his confines; victorious Viceroy of Egypt, the four corners of which shall be always respected and defended; so be it. And to all the distinguished princes, judges, men of learning and other officers whose business it is to maintain order and good government and to all commanders in general, may God preserve them in all their dignities, in the nobleness of their health!

'You are to know that our ancestors never bore any envy to other kings, nor did they ever occasion them any other trouble, or shew them any mark of hatred. On the contrary they have upon all occasions given them proof of their friendships, assisting them generously, relieving them in their necessities, as well as in what concerns the caravan and the pilgrims of Mecca in Arabia Felix, as in the Indies, in Persia and in other distant and out-of-the-way places, also by protecting distinguished persons in every urgent necessity.

'Nevertheless the king of France our brother, who professes our religion and our law, having been induced thereto by some advances of friendship on our part such as are proper, sent an ambassador to us. I understand that you caused arrest him at Sennaar, and also another by name Murat, the Syrian, whom you did put in prison also, though he was sent to that ambassador on our part, and by thus doing you have violated the law of nations, as ambassadors of kings ought to be at liberty to go wherever they will, and it is a general obligation to treat them with honour and not to molest or detain them, nor should they be subject to pay customs or any sort of presents.

We could very soon repay you in kind, if we were inclined to revenge the insult you have offered to the man Murat sent on our part; the Nile would be sufficient to punish you, since God hath put into our power his fountain, his outlet and his increase, and that we can dispose of the same to do you harm. For the present we demand of and exhort you to desist from any future vexations towards our envoys, and not disturb us by detaining those who shall be sent towards you, but you shall let them pass and continue their route without delay, coming and going wherever they will freely for their own advantage, whether they are our subjects or Frenchmen, and whatever you shall do to them or for them, we regard as done to or for ourselves.'

Du Roule was long dead by the time this letter was written, but it is not recorded that Takla Haymanot fulfilled the threat contained in it.

Takla Haymanot was after a short and undistinguished reign assassinated by a conspiracy of the nobility. He was succeeded by his uncle Theophilus. Theophilus took vengeance on those who had conspired against his brother Jesus and his nephew Takla Haymanot with equal severity and shortly afterwards died. On his death (1709) a revolution took place. The power of the nobility, not sufficiently severely checked during the long and merciful reign of Jesus, had increased inordinately during the two short reigns which followed. The nobles now set aside the royal house of Solomon, which had reigned without interruption since 1270, and proclaimed as king one of themselves, Justus, governor of Tigré and ras of the kingdom. Justus had a short and uneasy reign. The nobles who had raised him to the throne were jealous of him and conspiracies were soon formed. The people detested him as a usurper, and he increased his unpopularity by harbouring a number of Catholic priests who had smuggled themselves into the country. In 1714 he fell ill and, when it was heard that the nobles were planning to make his son king, the army lost patience and broke into revolt, proclaiming David son of Jesus king. David entered Gondar in triumph, and amidst universal rejoicings the line of Solomon was restored. One of David's first and most popular acts was the execution of the Catholic priests whom Justus had protected.

David survived his elevation to the throne only five years. He was a vehement champion of the Eustathian sect and fought a bitter feud with the monks of Debra Libanos. At length, irritated beyond measure by their insolence, he set his Galla troops on to them and massacred them. He was poisoned shortly after. On his death yet another son of Jesus the Great, 'Asma Giorgis, was proclaimed king by the army. He is better known by his nickname Bakaffa, which means the inexorable. He fully deserved the name. He set himself to break the power of the nobility. He ruthlessly suppressed conspiracy after conspiracy, and eventually he got all the important offices and governorships into the hands of trusted men of his own making. Despite his ruthless severity, or perhaps because of it, he has become a very popular figure in Abyssinian folk history, of which he is the Harun al Rashid. Many strange tales are told of him. He played on his subjects the age-old trick of pretending to be dead, and when his enemies had shown their hand reappearing and crushing them. He made a practice of wandering about the country in disguise in order to discover what people thought of his rule and who his rivals were likely to be. It was on one of these trips that he met his queen—unlike most Abyssinian kings he took one wife only. He fell sick of a fever in a village on the borders of Sennaar. The lord of the village kindly took him in and his daughter, Berhan Mugasa, 'the Glory of Grace', nursed him. She was worthy of her name, and on his return to Gondar Bakaffa summoned her and married her. On another journey Bakaffa met a young man washing his cloak in a pool. He was weary and sat down to rest and asked the young man to wash his cloak also. While he waited he questioned the young man on political affairs. He was very reticent, and at length being further pressed by the king he indignantly threw him back his cloak, saying, 'I thought when you prayed me to take your cloak that I was doing a charitable action to some poor Galla; but I have found you an instructor of kings and nobles. Take your cloak and wash it yourself; it is a safer trade and you will have less time to censure your superiors, which is not a proper occupation for a fellow like you.' Bakaffa was greatly pleased with this speech and presently summoned the speaker to Gondar and gave him high commands. He proved to be one of the king's most trusty and able adherents. His name was Waragna and he was a Galla by race. On another trip he saw an old man throwing sticks into a pool and foretelling the future from them. He asked what the sticks said, and the old man said that their message was that the king would have a son but that one called Wallata Giorgis who was no kin of the king should govern the kingdom for thirty years after the king's death. Bakaffa was greatly perturbed and set about killing the numerous persons who bore this not uncommon name. Presently the queen bore him a son, and, his anxiety being renewed, he told her the prophecy. She laughed and said, 'This Wallata Giorgis is even now with you in the palace'. The king leapt to his feet in horror and the queen then said: 'My name by baptism was Wallata Giorgis, and if you should die leaving an infant son, I would rule the kingdom though none of your kin.'[1]

[1] These stories were told to Bruce by the queen herself, who was still alive some forty years later. There may therefore be some historical foundation in them.

ii. THE COLLAPSE OF THE MONARCHY

The prophecy was duly fulfilled. Bakaffa died after a ten years' reign in 1729, and the queen, having summoned her four brothers and the faithful Galla, Waragna, to her aid, had her infant son, Jesus II, proclaimed king without opposition. During the long reign of Jesus II (1729–53) the power of the Solomonian line fell into its final decline. The queen-mother made herself extremely unpopular among the nobility by putting all the best posts in the hands of her own relatives. At the same time she was not strong enough to crush the numerous conspiracies and rebellions in which the discontent of the nobility manifested itself. She had to compromise, and thus the power of the nobles, temporarily checked by her husband, reasserted itself. Jesus himself, when he came of age, proved a dilettante. He was greatly addicted to hunting. He also had artistic tastes which he indulged at great expense. A recent persecution had caused a large number of Greeks to flee from Smyrna. They sought refuge in Abyssinia and Jesus, finding that they were skilled craftsmen, gave them a warm welcome. With their aid he began rebuilding his palace on a magnificent scale. Bruce saw the rooms, still unfinished and by that time falling into ruin, and admired them greatly. The walls were wainscoted in ivory, their upper part was covered with Venetian mirrors, bought at vast expense; the wooden ceiling was very richly carved and painted. Jesus bestowed great estates on his Smyrniot favourites and spent nearly all his time visiting them. Not unnaturally the people began to be discontented with their king. He was nicknamed Jesus the Little, in contrast to his grandfather, Jesus the Great, and mock annals were composed, recording his glorious expeditions to the houses of his Smyrniots. Jesus was stung by these lampoons and led his army to conquer Sennaar. The campaign was a disastrous failure, nearly the whole of the Abyssinian army being destroyed. At this point the abuna died and Jesus, having spent all his money on Venetian mirrors, had to levy a tax on the churches to pay the expenses of obtaining a new abuna. The mission for the new abuna proved a most disastrous and expensive affair. The naib of Massaua first pocketed all the money that had been meant for the authorities in Cairo. The mission was then forced to land at Jidda, where the Sharif of Mecca demanded and obtained an equal sum. When the new abuna finally arrived at Massaua he was imprisoned by the naib, but was fortunately smuggled out of prison and got into Abyssinia by the ingenuity of a Greek agent of the king. Jesus was furious at this episode. He knew that the naib would never have dared to behave with such insolence without the connivance of Michael Suhul, the governor of Tigré, who had him completely under his thumb. He summoned Michael to Gondar to account for his conduct. Michael refused point blank. Jesus marched against him, defeated him and apparently had him at his mercy. But the nobility all pleaded for the life of one of their own number—Michael had incidentally distributed a large share of his great wealth among them—and Jesus weakly consented to spare him. Later, with incredible folly, he restored him to his province and added several more to it. Michael Suhul was now the most powerful man in the kingdom. He ruled all Abyssinia north of the Takazzé. He was the virtual ruler of Massaua and thus controlled all the external trade of Abyssinia. He made a very great profit out of the customs. He also controlled the import of firearms into Abyssinia and was able to arm his troops in a far more efficient manner than the king or any of the other governors. He now bided his time. He had narrowly escaped destruction once by allowing himself to be drawn into a struggle while the prestige of the monarchy still stood and he himself had not consolidated himself strongly enough. He had managed to extricate himself from his difficulties by a prudent use of his wealth and the exercise of his great talents for intrigue. He was now waiting for the royal family to complete its own ruin.

It did so soon. The queen-mother, jealous of the power of the nobles, had married her son to a Galla wife, named Wobit. When Jesus died in 1753, still a young man despite his long reign, the old queen-mother found herself ousted by Wobit, who ruled in the name of her young son, Joas. A Galla supremacy now began. Wobit had brought with her a large force of her tribesmen when she first arrived. Bakaffa's faithful Galla minister, Waragna, was already governor of Damot, and on his death, soon after Joas's accession, his tribesmen proclaimed his son Fasil governor, killing the king's uncle who had been sent to succeed him. Wobit now summoned her two brothers, Lubo and Brulhé, to court; each brought a large bodyguard of Gallas with him. Lubo was appointed governor of Amhara, but the popular resentment was so great that the appointment had to be withdrawn. Undeterred, Joas appointed his other uncle, Brulhé, governor of Begamedr. The idea of entrusting this key-province to a Galla and his savage followers horrified the whole people. The existing governor refused to move, saying that he had sworn on his appointment never to admit the Gallas to his province. Brulhé attacked him and was defeated and killed. Joas was now reduced to a desperate position and he called upon Michael Suhul to assist him, conferring upon him the position of ras of the kingdom.

Michael now had the game in his hands. He occupied Gondar in force. In order to complete the king's unpopu-

THE COLLAPSE OF THE MONARCHY

larity he consented, under protest, to crush the rebellious and highly popular governor of Begamedr. He then turned against the remnants of the Galla faction, now led by Fasil, Waragna's son, in Damot. In this he was not so successful. He defeated Fasil but did not crush him. Finding that Joas had been secretly supporting Fasil he promptly had him murdered, and procured from Amba Wahni a son of Jesus the Great named John. John was over seventy and proved too feeble even for Ras Michael's purposes. He was poisoned after a few months and his son, Takla Haymanot, was put on the throne. It was at this juncture that Bruce arrived in Abyssinia.

Bruce's picture of Abyssinia in its period of decadence is, despite his racy style, depressing. The kingdom had shrunk greatly in extent. The area which the king would have controlled if there had been no rebellion at the moment—and at any given moment there always was a rebellion—did not extend farther south than the Abai. All touch had been lost with the surviving islands of Christian population in the sea of roving Gallas. In the south-east Shoa was virtually an independent kingdom, ruled by hereditary governors. It still owed an ill-defined allegiance to the Crown, and while Bruce was in Gondar the governor of Shoa sent a present of gold and a body of horse to assist Takla Haymanot. This was, however, a very exceptional event and caused great excitement. The governors of Shoa had effectively cut themselves off from contact with the rest of the kingdom by planting the Wollo tribe of the Gallas on their northern frontier. Behind this screen they lived undisturbed by the turmoils of the rest of the kingdom and taking little part in them. They were an able dynasty, and it is from them that the present royal house of Abyssinia is descended. The other governorships also tended to be hereditary, but the frequent reshufflings due to the civil wars prevented the formation of any permanent dynasties.

Except for the Gallas, Abyssinia had no dangerous enemies. The once powerful Moslem kingdoms of Somaliland had sunk into insignificance. With the decline of the Ottoman Empire the Turkish occupation of Massaua had become a mere name. The pashalik had been abolished and the command of the town had been given to the chief of the local Beja tribe. He paid an annual tribute to the Sublime Porte and received in return a firman of appointment under the title of naib. The Turkish garrison still received pay from Constantinople, but by many generations of intermarriage with the natives they had long ceased to bear any resemblance to Turks or to soldiers; Bruce gives an amusing picture of the ragged crowd of savages who still bore the proud title of Janissaries. The Abyssinians could easily have crushed this pitiful parody of a Turkish governor and garrison, but the governors of Tigré found it more convenient to maintain it and use it as an excuse for exactions from which they took their percentage.

In many ways the life of the country was unchanged. The Church was still much the same as ever. The country was still thickly studded with churches and monasteries, priests and monks still abounded and the abuna was still attended by hordes of candidates for holy orders, whom he ordained in huge batches. Catholics were still hated and theological disputes ran high—one of the first questions asked of Bruce was 'Had Christ two natures or one?' Despite the practical impotence of the monarchy the king was still surrounded with a certain state. He was never seen to set foot upon the ground outside his palace. He rode right into his presence chamber, and when he went to church, which he did on foot, the road to the church and the church itself were cleared for his benefit. On formal occasions, at audiences, and when he sat in judgement, his face was veiled. He likewise never spoke on formal occasions; an officer styled the Voice of the King was his mouthpiece. He sat in judgement every day before breakfast in the court of the palace. The palace was always surrounded by large crowds, shouting 'O king, give us justice', and so essential was this for his dignity that if, owing to wet weather, genuine litigants were scarce vagabonds were hired to take up the cry. The custom applied to all great men as Bruce found to his great annoyance when he was appointed a governor. At meetings of the council of state the king sat in a kind of box, surveying the other members, who sat round a table, through a grill. The members of the council, which consisted of the commanders of the royal army, various officers of the household, the principal governors of provinces, the Keeper of the Hour, the chamberlain, and the ras, gave their opinions in that order—that is in inverse order of precedence—and finally the king communicated his decision through the Voice of the King. All these ceremonies must have been a trifle ridiculous when the king lodged in a few derelict rooms of a half-ruined palace. Large parts of Basilides' palace at Gondar had been burnt down from time to time in revolutions, and Jesus II's magnificent rooms lay unfinished with most of their Venetian mirrors smashed.

Justice was as rough and ready as ever, and punishments were more brutal. Mutilations such as tearing out the eyes or cutting off one arm or leg were regular penalties. The bodies of persons convicted of treason were not allowed to be buried but were thrown into the streets. Owing to the frequent convictions for treason in these troubled times the streets were often littered with fragments of corpses left by the hyaenas; these beasts haunted the town at night and made it dangerous to go out after dark.

The army was still to a very large extent armed in the medieval manner with swords and spears; bows had been abandoned. A very small proportion was armed with muskets. The king's regular army consisted nominally of about eight thousand men, of whom a quarter bore firearms. He had also a bodyguard of sixteen hundred men—at full strength, which it rarely was; these were almost entirely foreigners, Gallas and negro slaves for the most part. Many of the provincial governors also maintained standing armies, often more numerous and better equipped than that of the king. General levies were summoned for special campaigns. The king issued three successive proclamations on these occasions: first, 'Buy your mules, get ready your provisions and pay your servants, for after such and such a day they that seek me here shall not find me', then, a few days later, 'Cut down the thorns in the four quarters of the world, for I know not where I am going', and finally, 'I am encamped in such and such a place; him that does not join me there I will chastise for seven years.'

Bruce tells in detail the history of the five years that he was in Abyssinia. He tells how Michael again attacked Fasil, again without decisive success, how the governors of Amhara and Begamedr, jealous of Michael, plotted with Fasil to destroy him, how Michael withdrew with the king to his own province of Tigré, how the governors of Amhara and Begamedr set up a rival king in Gondar, how Fasil quarrelled with them and was reconciled with Michael, how Michael returned in triumph to Gondar, how the other three again combined to overthrow him and so forth and so on. Such unending intrigues and civil wars were to be the history of Abyssinia for the next hundred years, till the line of Solomon, long the plaything of ambitious governors, came to an inglorious end, and new kings arose to restore unity with a strong hand.

PART V

i. 1770–1870. THE STRUGGLE AMONG THE GREAT CHIEFS

JAMES BRUCE left Abyssinia about 1772. His friendship with Michael had preserved him there through the troubles of five years, but in the end the spectacles it involved became unbearable. 'I at last scarce ever went out', he wrote, 'and nothing occupied my thoughts but how to escape from this bloody country.'

In the end he achieved his escape by a terrible route along the Blue Nile to Sennaar and through Nubia, only to have doubts cast, once in London, on the gruesome and often fantastic stories he brought home. Deeply offended, he retired to nurse his grievances in Scotland. But a later generation gives him the praise he deserves for his work as a traveller and scholar, for the vast knowledge he acquired of Abyssinian manners and history, and for some valuable manuscripts which permit other scholars to lift the curtain and study a queer and rather harrowing scene.

The quarrels among the rases and the enthronement and deposition of their rival puppets as emperor lasted for a hundred years. By 1800 the tempo had accelerated to such a pace that there were said to be no less than six emperors living. It is small wonder that Mr. Henry Salt, a member of Lord Valentia's party which surveyed the Red Sea in 1805, was at a loss with whom to leave the presents and letters to the emperor by His Majesty King George III. One chief seemed as good as another, and, failing to penetrate to Gondar, he left them with the ras of Tigré.

In the early eighteen-hundreds the principals in the struggle had been reduced to four: the rulers of Tigré, in the north-east; of Amhara, who controlled the titular emperor at Gondar; of Gojjam, just south of Lake Tsana, and of Shoa, farther to the east. In the years round 1850 a surfeit of civil wars brought about the simultaneous death of two of these, Ali of Gondar and Goshu of Gojjam, and paved the way to the dominance of one of the two survivors. But it was a third party who entered the field and became *Negusa Nagast*, or King of Kings, in 1855.

Kassa, later King Theodore, had had a remarkable life. He was born in about 1818; his father, reputed to belong to the Queen of Sheba's royal line, was a minor chief in Kwara. On his death his small fortune was seized by relations, and his widow was left so poor that she was obliged to sell *kosso*, a drug advocated in Abyssinia as a specific against the tapeworm, in the streets of Gondar. The young Kassa was brought up first in a monastery on Lake Tsana, and later in the house of a soldierly but scheming uncle. He next became a kind of highwayman in the lowlands, and was known as the scourge of the Moslem merchants who plied on the caravan route towards the Nile. Malcontents and adventurers joined his band; finally he became so powerful in his district as to excite the jealousy of the queen-mother of Gondar, who dispatched an army to crush 'the kosso-vendor's son'. The expedition failed and Ali, ras of Gondar, decided to confirm him in the possession of the province he had overrun, and, in 1847, to give him his daughter to wife.

The civil wars which followed lifted Kassa from strength to strength. By 1854 he was ruler of both Gondar and Gojjam, and his only serious rivals were the ras of Tigré and the king of Shoa. Both these were sufficiently powerful to aspire to the imperial crown, and the former, on hearing of the death of the old ras of Gondar, at once had himself proclaimed King of Kings. The abuna was on his way to Tigré for the coronation when he was intercepted by Kassa, and, after parleys, came to terms. If Kassa would consent to expel all the Roman Catholic missionaries, he, the abuna, would crown him and not the ras of Tigré. Kassa agreed to this, and later kept his word, leaving the abuna the task of convincing his retinue of clergy that Kassa had become the Chosen of God—not difficult since they were surrounded by Kassa's army, already showing signs of impatience.

War with Tigré followed, but Kassa, who had the advantage of possessing what amounted to a standing army inspired by personal attachment to him, was again victorious, and took his rival prisoner; two days later he was crowned, on February 7, 1855. He chose the throne-name of Theodore, believing himself to be destined to fulfil the legend that a just and righteous king of that name would one day wipe out Islam, conquer Jerusalem, and occupy the throne of Solomon.

The extraordinary saga of Theodore's rise to power has been told by his two English friends, John Bell and Walter Chichele Plowden. Plowden, a young merchantman in a Calcutta office, decided in 1843, when twenty-three years old, that he disliked a sedentary life. He threw up his post and embarked for England by the overland route via Suez. Here he fell in with John Bell, who persuaded him, on the spur of the moment and with limited funds, to join him on an expedition into Abyssinia. In 1847, the stories with which he returned to England persuaded Lord Palmerston that a mission to Gondar was called for, and in 1848 Plowden returned to the court of Ali, ras of Gondar, with whom he concluded a trade treaty in 1849. The ras, upon signing it, remarked that it would do no good as he was certain that no English merchant would ever come to Abyssinia; it proved as futile as he predicted.

When Theodore conquered Gondar in 1854, both Plowden and Bell transferred their allegiance to him and remained at his court until their deaths at the time of the Tigré rebellion of 1860. John Bell died fighting at the emperor's side; Plowden was murdered when, broken in health, he was making his way to the coast and home to England through the unruly north.

One of Theodore's first acts was to depose the libertine John III, last of the titular emperors, and to transfer his capital from Gondar in the west to Magdala on the eastern edge of the highlands. Here he fortified the town and restored the altars and churches which marauding Gallas had laid waste during the civil wars among the Christian tribes.

The War Office map of Abyssinia published as the frontispiece to Plowden's book, and Plowden's own map of the northern provinces, give a good idea of the empire of Theodore's day. 'The noble portion of territory still in the possession of the Christians of Eastern Africa', says Plowden, 'is blessed with a climate that may, perhaps, challenge comparison with any in the world.' It consisted of Amhara, Gojjam, and Shoa, and, to the north, of subject provinces stretching beyond Tigré to the Red Sea coast. Towards its west the Shankallas, 'bloodthirsty to a degree', inhabited lower country where 'elephants, rhinoceroses, buffaloes, lions, camelopards, and ostriches abound, besides half a dozen large kinds of antelopes'. On the east, where the Tigré and Amhara mountains fall almost perpendicularly to the scorched plain, were the fierce but prosperous Danakils, tending 'the fattest cows and sheep I ever met with out of England'. Ringed round the highlands, on the south and east, were tribe after tribe of rival Gallas, a 'nation of horsemen', whose local boundaries formed 'an uncultivated battle-ground where, driving their cows to graze, they dispute the pasturage in daily combats'. At times these Moslem Gallas were subject to the sway of one ras or another; at others, the Abyssinians were too feeble or too busy to hold them, leaving them free to expend their energy on private war or raids into the highlands.

Theodore, on his accession, set himself three aims: to break the power of the nobles, to destroy or convert the Gallas, and to expel all Moslems who would not adopt the Christian faith. He had in him enough of the *führer* or the *duce* to fit him almost ideally for the task; in particular he was brave, and possessed of a fanatical zeal—in his case, for Christianity. His advantages over his fellow chiefs were his large personal following, dating from his bandit days, and the education which he owed to his training as a scribe in the Tsana monastery, and which caused him to devise the modern system of breaking up the provinces into smaller units under governors appointed by himself. His undoing was his temper. 'The worst points in his character', noted Plowden, 'are his violent anger at times and his unyielding pride as regards his kingly and divine right.'

Up till 1860 he was at the height of his power. He had captured Shoa without a blow, and had kindly treated the young prince Menelik whom he took captive. He had been moderately successful against the Gallas and had quelled a formidable rebellion in Tigré. But after the death of his two English friends, Plowden and Bell, he seemed to become possessed of a sort of *folie de grandeur*. He gave rein to his worst instincts, over-indulged in liquor, lived openly with a Galla concubine, and disgusted 'even the Gallas'. Losing his hold over the army, he was reduced to killing and burning alive thousands in a desperate attempt to save his face by his frightfulness.

News from Abyssinia filtered slowly to Europe, if at

all; ignorant of this degeneracy, the British Government decided that Plowden must have a successor. Thus, in 1862, Captain Cameron arrived on a scene of chaotic slaughter rather incongruously bearing a letter from Queen Victoria thanking the Negus for ransoming Plowden's body. Accompanying the letter were a rifle and a pair of pistols, and a letter and a decoration from Prince Albert. Theodore thanked Cameron, and told him that he had already executed 1,500 men of the tribe responsible for Plowden's death; he added that his policy was to crush the Turks and the Egyptians. Next, writing as one Christian sovereign to another, he suggested to Queen Victoria and to the Emperor Napoleon an Abyssinian embassy to Great Britain and France respectively.

The oversight by which the British Foreign Office pigeon-holed this letter proved most expensive, for it cost Great Britain the expedition to Magdala in 1868. When dispatches arrived from England early in 1864 Theodore at once asked for the answer from Queen Victoria; there was none. He took this as a gross personal insult to himself and his nation. His wrath burst like a bomb on the head of poor Cameron, who with certain other Englishmen was thrown into prison. Matters were not improved when the British Government sent a Levantine, Mr. Hormuzd Rassam, to obtain the release of the prisoners. In 1866, obeying a sudden whim, Theodore seized Rassam also, and placed him and some sixty other Europeans in iron anklets and fetters. He then locked both consignments of prisoners into his fortress at Magdala.

The rescuing expedition under Sir Robert Napier landed at Annesley Bay—just south of the present Italian port of Massaua—in 1867. Its first problem was water. A series of drawings in the contemporary *Illustrated London News* show the measures taken to combat shortage. One shows a top-hatted group experimenting, against a background of the shires, with 'Norton's patent tube-wells, an American invention for extracting water from the ground'; the next, men and animals drinking at tanks specially built at the base; the next a condensing plant on the shore; the next, a cumbersome operation with suction and chain pumps at the mouth of a mountain pass.

The even more formidable problem of advancing into a country whose mountains and gorges constituted a vast natural fortress was unwittingly solved by Theodore himself. Realizing that his power was on the wane he had in 1866 made a desperate effort to humour the army by allowing it to devastate fourteen provinces. This wantonness was his undoing, and Napier found plenty of willing native helpers all along his road to Magdala. Nevertheless, his march, carried out with elephants, camels, mules, and oxen was something of a feat, plunging as it had to do from camps eight or ten thousand feet above sea-level into deep jungle-choked gorges, ravines impassable with mud, and passes which could be held by a handful of determined defenders. Some idea of the difficulties can be gained from the fact that though Magdala was only 325 miles from the Red Sea base, the expedition took nearly a year.

Napier encountered Theodore's army at Arogee on April 10, 1868. The Abyssinians, charging down the mountain side into an open valley, were mown down in lines by the British fire. Though they were obviously appalled at this first taste of modern weapons, their reckless bravery is commented upon by every eyewitness; the remnant retired in good order, cheering as they went. Theodore, who had remained on the heights to direct the artillery fire, went down to meet them on the lower slopes. He called out for general after general, but none answered. Knowing then that defeat was inevitable, he retired to Magdala. The

British troops followed. He shot himself as they entered the town on Easter Monday, 1868.

A document which he sent to Sir Robert Napier just before his death throws light on the character of a very remarkable man:

'O, people of Abyssinia, will it always be thus that you flee before the enemy when I myself, by the Power of God, go not forth with you to encourage you?

'Believing myself to be a great lord, I gave you battle; but by reason of the worthlessness of my artillery, all my pains were as naught.

'Out of what I have done of evil towards my people may God bring good. His Will be done. I had intended, if God had so decreed, to conquer the whole world; and it was my desire to die if my purpose could not be fulfilled.'

Napier made no attempt to settle the succession. He freed the political prisoners, among them the gluttonous old Emperor John III, who had lived for years in captivity, but he wisely turned a deaf ear to John's plea for restoration to the throne. His object had been the rescue of the captives and, this achieved, he began his march back to the coast, his only spoils being a gold chalice, the abuna's crown, the gold crown of King Theodore, and the royal copy of the *Kebra Nagast*.[1] He left Abyssinian territory at the end of May 1868, and for four years the country was plunged back into the old-time struggle between the chieftains.

ii. 1870–1916. THE EMPERORS VERSUS THE POWERS

In 1872 the ras of Tigré emerged triumphant from the struggle and was crowned emperor with the title of John IV.

[1] The story of the *Kebra Nagast* has already been told (page 20); the chalice is now in the Victoria and Albert Museum, London. Theodore's crown was returned to Abyssinia by King George V, in 1925, the bearer being Ras Tafari (now the Emperor Haile Selassie).

The northern mountains of Abyssinia—an air photograph, showing the heavy-wooded slopes and plateau cultivation. (From the Wardour Film, *Abyssinia*)

The new Negus was as brave as Theodore, and possessed his virtues but none of his vices; but he was never given an opportunity to show his ability to develop the country. The travellers of his generation were no longer free lances like Bruce and Plowden, but bagmen with machines and western devices made in Birmingham and Leipzig and Lille and Brussels, and with a supply of blank treaty-forms in their luggage. Through the whole of his reign he was almost ceaselessly distracted by the aspirations, military and commercial, of outside powers.

The first to disturb him was Egypt. Khedive Said had in 1863 been succeeded by the more ambitious Khedive Ismail, who harboured plans for the conquest of Abyssinia. By 1872 he had seized the whole of the Red Sea shore from under the shadowy suzerainty of Turkey, and by 1875 he had encircled John's territory on the east and south, and had occupied Berbera and Harar. He decided to attack John from the north, but the Abyssinians, fighting in the mountain country which suited them best, routed his two expeditions in 1875 and 1876.

The Egyptian front was quiet until the revolt of Arabi Pasha in 1882 led to the bombardment of Alexandria and the British occupation. The Mahdist rebellion followed, and by 1883 all the Sudan south of Khartum was in the hands of the Dervishes. These disturbing neighbours did not worry John at first; indeed, their victory might well prove an advantage, for on the strength of it the British—on whom the death of Gordon at Khartum in 1884 seemed to make a disheartening impression—advised the Egyptians to abandon all their southern conquests. When they evacuated Harar and the coast, it looked as if the obstacles to Abyssinian aggrandizement were melting unaided.

But they went only to be replaced by another menace. The opening of the Suez Canal in 1869 had turned the

Red Sea from a cul-de-sac into a highway and had given a new importance to the coast. The scramble for Africa was beginning, and the powers were becoming practised at unfurling flags. The unwitting John was launched into the middle of an eternal triangle: Britain, France, Italy. But the real struggle for Abyssinian independence, growing more vital as these three settled more comfortably into their colonial bases, was to fall to his successor, the Emperor Menelik.

Escaping from his captivity in Magdala during one of Theodore's orgies, Menelik had returned to Shoa and re-established himself on the throne. He ignored the struggles in the north by which John fought his way to the emperorship, and, acting on French advice, methodically set about conquering the rich Galla country to the south and west of his kingdom. He bought modern equipment for his troops, and French adventurers did a roaring trade in out-of-date small arms which they bought in Europe for five or six francs and sold in Shoa for forty. According to the accounts of the poet Rimbaud, who was one such trader, quick profits were to be had for the asking.

Menelik's object was permanent conquest, not mere raiding, and he therefore garrisoned the towns he captured with Shoan troops who exempted the Gallas from massacre only in return for tribute and military service. The French advice proved good, and John, fearing Menelik's increasing power, thought it wise to come to terms. In 1882 they agreed on their respective territories; Menelik was to have Harar, Kaffa, and the Galla countries, John the more northerly territory of the Wollo Gallas. At the same time they arranged a marriage between John's son of twelve and Menelik's daughter Zauditu, aged seven, and stipulated in the marriage contract that Menelik should succeed John as King of Kings. Though the Emperor, just before his death in 1889, broke this undertaking by nominating his natural son, Ras Mangasha of Tigré, as his heir, Menelik, at the head of his Shoan army, was by then so powerful that Mangasha could scarcely contest his long-foreseen claim to the imperial throne.

Of his three European neighbours, by far the most pressing was Italy. Busy with unification at home, she had come to the African feast not only late but as a poor relation, and had been given as her share two coastal deserts, Somaliland and Eritrea.

In 1869 a private Italian company had bought a trading station called Assab at the northern end of the Straits of Bab-el-Mandeb; a few years later it was taken over by the Rubbatino Shipping Company, who found it a good starting-point for caravans travelling inland. In 1882 the Italian Government bought the port from the Company, and sent a mission to Menelik at Shoa to conclude a trade treaty and to obtain his help in improving their colony. In 1884 the British for a short time occupied the coast now known as Eritrea in order to evacuate certain Egyptian garrisons marooned by the Mahdi in the Sudan; they sought Abyssinian help by promising the Emperor John the ex-Egyptian territories behind Massaua. In 1885, their object achieved, the British left, at the same time encouraging and approving the Italians in the occupation of some further coastal towns, including Massaua, a move which brought them dangerously near to the newly promised boundaries of Tigré.

The landing of two Italian military expeditions at Massaua in February and March 1885 proved to John that the new arrivals had colonial expansion in view; they pushed inland with a succession of small forts and outposts, ostensibly to protect the caravan routes. Skirmishes with the Abyssinians began to take place on the northern border, and the ras of a Tigré tribe seized the members of a so-called 'scientific mission' which had penetrated some way into the highlands. A small Italian relief column of 500 men set out in 1887, but its task was far harder than that of the Magdala expedition, for, instead of help, it received every kind of hindrance from the local tribes. Coming up with an Abyssinian force of some 20,000 men, the Italians were practically exterminated at Dogali on January 26, 1887. The defeat resulted in the evacuation of all up-country outposts; the news caused consternation in Rome, and reinforcements were at once sent off to Massaua. The British, disturbed at the prospect of a war, sent Mr. Gerald Portal to Shoa to try and preserve the peace, but to no purpose. The Italians marched inland, but before any battle took place they seemed to decide on new tactics. They would bargain with Menelik against John.

In October 1888 they sent a mission to Shoa. Menelik was promised money and cartridges, the province of Tigré and recognition as King of Kings, provided he would help them to fight John, and would cede them Asmara and some land on the fringe of the uplands which would improve the value of their colony. Menelik accepted their munitions, against a rainy day, but did nothing. Action was superfluous. He was in the strongest of positions as the successor desired by both sides. He had only a year to wait before John's death from a stray Mahdist bullet in 1889 turned a victory over the Dervishes into an Abyssinian rout.

Menelik and the Italians both took advantage of the anarchy which followed. Fortunately for both, the Mahdi did not press home his victory and contented himself with seizing John's body and sending his sword in triumph to Omdurman. The Italians reoccupied their highland outposts, and helped Menelik to proclaim himself King of Kings.

1870-1916. THE EMPERORS VERSUS THE POWERS 139

He had no serious rival; being able to trace his descent from a daughter of King David (1508-40) he was a member of the House of Solomon; he was also the most outstanding personality among the rases; best argument of all, he had the Shoan army at his back. Ras Mangasha of Tigré, the only other possible claimant, had no such material advantage to offer.

The Italians at once signed with Menelik the Treaty of Ucciali. This gave Italy a virtual protectorate over the country, for by its terms, in the Italian text, Menelik 'consents to avail himself of the Italian Government for any negotiations which he may enter into with other Powers or Governments'. A month or so later Menelik's nephew, Ras Makonnen, the governor of Harar, was sent on a mission to Rome. By the supplementary treaty which he made there, the Italians were to lend Menelik 4,000,000 francs with the customs of Harar as security, and, failing repayment, the cession of the whole province of Harar to Italy. King Umberto made the ras a present of 28 cannon and 38,000 rifles—the weapons which were later to win the battle of Adowa—and Italy announced to the world that Abyssinia was an Italian protectorate.

In 1890, after crushing a rebellion in Tigré, where Ras Mangasha was making a last bid for the throne, Menelik on his own account began to open negotiations with other Powers, and received both French and Russian emissaries. The Italians protested; Count Antonelli was sent post-haste to the Abyssinian court; this, he said, was a breach of the Treaty of Ucciali. But Menelik argued no: the wording of the Italian text was beside the point; the Amharic text, the only copy signed, clearly stated not that Menelik 'consents to use' but that he 'may use' the Italians as intermediaries. He contended that his was the option, and he stood his ground. Over the next three years he grew gradually more and more incensed at the activities of the Italians in the consolidation of their colony—in 1890 christened Eritrea. In 1893, hoping to induce his acquiescence in their protectorate, they made him a present of 2,000,000 cartridges. This was the last straw; Menelik kept the cartridges but paid back in full the money he had received on loan. His position thus thoroughly fortified, he denounced the Treaty of Ucciali.

Eritrea was not Italy's only portion in Africa. In 1885 His Majesty's ship *Barbarigo* of the Royal Italian Navy had been dispatched round the corner of Cape Gardafui to explore the mouth of the Juba river and to join in the treaty-making on which the British and the Germans were already engaged with the Sultan of Zanzibar. Italy, too, secured a treaty. In 1888 another expedition landed at Obbia (now in Italian Somaliland), and with the Sultan's permission established a protectorate; another agreement extended this benefit northward to the Mijjertein. Italy notified these arrangements to the Powers. In the next year, Captain Filonardi arrived with two more men-of-war and a new mission, and by 1891 the Italian flag was flying at most of the landing stages from Cape Gardafui along the Somaliland and Benadir coast to the Juba river. In 1893 the Government leased the Benadir to a company, but, as penetration inland went on, a commercial concern proved poor at managing the wild tribes with which it had to deal. The crux came with the campaign against the Mad Mullah, which was fought over the Italian-Somali hinterland in the first years of the twentieth century. The inadequacies of the Company became evident and in 1905 the Italian Government took over the colony.

Menelik was unaffected by these Italian plans; he was probably unaware that they were going on, for between Harar and the Benadir coast lay the country of the Ogaden, a waterless tract covered with thorn and so-called high 'grass', and too low and hot to suit the Abyssinian constitution. Even the Gallas preferred higher ground.

The British and the French, in their Somaliland settlements, were less remote, and both had dealings with Shoa. Menelik found them easier to treat with than the Italians, mainly because both were digesting vast new possessions elsewhere and so were less acquisitive than Italy. This frame of mind is revealed in a resolution appearing in the minute book of a House of Commons committee in 1865:

'That all further extension of territory or assumption of government or new treaty offering any protection to native tribes would be inexpedient.'

Therefore, though the British had been on the coast opposite Aden since about 1840 (when the East India Company had bought for ten bags of rice a place 'for the harbour of their ships without any prohibition whatsoever'), they had never tried to penetrate towards Harar and Shoa. Their missions into Abyssinia had been purely utilitarian—to rescue the captives in Magdala or the Egyptian garrisons from the Mahdi—and had been abandoned as soon as the immediate object had been achieved. 'On our side,' Lord Edward Gleichen writes of Napier's exploit, 'having spent an immense sum of money with an extremely inadequate return for it—for the country which we had conquered, Northern Abyssinia, was commercially valueless and not worth annexing—we were content to let the matter drop.'

But this casualness turned to concern when the Mahdist victories in 1884 caused the withdrawal of the Egyptians from Harar. The British, suddenly uncertain as to the future of the hinterland, began to make treaties first with the Somalis, then with the French, then with the Italians. The agreements which they signed with the latter are interesting because, though now anachronisms, they are still valid to-day. Those of importance were signed in 1891 when the Treaty of Ucciali was still in full force and Abyssinia in the eyes of the world an Italian protectorate. They defined the respective spheres of influence of the two Powers in East Africa, and allocated practically the whole of Abyssinia to the Italian sphere. So little was known of the uplands that the Nile water supply—later to become Britain's predominant interest—was not even mentioned.

The French, though without territorial designs, had paid far more attention to Abyssinian politics than had the British. They therefore realized the full significance of every development, particularly of the Italian moves towards the uplands. It was at their instigation that Menelik first pointed out to the Italians the discrepancy in the two texts of the Treaty of Ucciali. Next, again acting on their advice, he wrote a circular letter to the European Powers stating the exact limits of his Empire: 'I shall endeavour, should God of his grace grant me the years and the strength, to restore the ancient frontiers of Ethiopia as far as Khartum and to Lake Nyanza beyond the lands of the Galla.' This remarkable document, dated April 1891—the month in which the Anglo-Italian agreement parcelled out the same territory—was never circulated; possibly Menelik gave it to his Italian allies to post.

But the chief French interest was commercial and centred round the idea of a railway which would turn their port at Jibuti into the principal outlet for Abyssinia. In 1894 a Paris syndicate successfully negotiated a ninety-nine year concession for the line. The traffic outlook was promising; Paris speculators began to take up the shares.

It was some time before they saw a return for their money, for the Italian menace in the north was growing so pressing that Menelik had no time to pay attention to prospectors in the Eastern lowlands.

Menelik had always had reason to doubt the loyalty of Ras Mangasha of Tigré, his rival for the crown of the King of Kings. In 1891 he discovered him to be treaty-making with the Italians, and, in return for support, undertaking to rebel and detach Tigré from the Abyssinian empire. The contract was not very creditable to either side, as the Italians were still bound to Menelik by the Treaty of Ucciali. Then for two years they paid no attention to Mangasha, for their new general, Baratieri, was busy with a brilliant campaign against the Dervishes; they paid dearly for this temporary deflection of their interest from the politics of Tigré.

In 1895 Ras Mangasha, tiring of an alliance which seemed to be bringing him no good, threw in his lot with Menelik, and marched north. He took no notice of Baratieri's order that he should disband, and the Italians, who were dependent on a timid ministry at home, were too short of men and funds to take a strong line with him. Baratieri hurried back to Rome and succeeded in rousing the Government from its lethargy; he secured money and supplies and returned to the colony. But he had made two bad miscalculations; he underestimated the quality of Menelik's troops and he counted on help from the insurgent rases. This did not materialize. Menelik had in September 1895 issued a proclamation about the foreign menace which raised a wave of genuine patriotism among the tribes. It brought all his vassals to his side, and the army with which he awaited the Italian invasion included his own Shoan soldiers, the Harar troops under the faithful Ras Makonnen, Ras Mangasha's men from Tigré, the Gojjam army, and the Galla cavalry.

Baratieri, fresh from Rome, knew that his whole reputation was staked on the campaign. One story runs that he knew he was to be superseded by a senior officer, and determined to win his laurels before he was obliged to hand over the command. But it is unlikely that the news of his supersession, announced in Rome only on February 22, should have reached him in the mountains before the battle. At all events, Crispi, the foreign minister, had telegraphed peremptory orders for an 'authentic victory'. Baratieri decided upon a surprise attack on Adowa, the capital of Tigré, choosing Sunday, March 1, 1896, a feast day in the Abyssinian Church, when he hoped that the armies would have gone to worship at the holy city of Axum.

He had no idea of the size of the enemy force; it passed belief that Menelik could move so many troops so fast over the ground he had to cover. He also believed his Italians to be so far superior in equipment that he could repeat Napier's victory; he had counted without the plentiful ammunition which Menelik had for some years been importing through Jibuti, not to mention some Hotchkiss quick-firing mountain guns which the Abyssinians, far nimbler than the Italians, were able to move swiftly from point to point of vantage. But his real undoing was the faultiness of his local maps.

Leaving his camp at nightfall on February 29 (it was leap year), he advanced with 14,500 men in three columns towards Adowa. It had been raining all day and the going was slow and heavy. He intended to occupy three hills commanding the Adowa plain; his left wing, consisting of native troops under General Albertone, was to make the longest circuit and to take its station on that farthest to the south, marked Chidane Meret. Albertone's men far outdistanced the two Italian detachments, and when he took up his place at daybreak there were no signs of the central force which should have lain to his right. He sent back runners; none returned. Then his native guides told him that the hill he was on was wrongly mapped; the real Chidane Meret was some miles on. Seriously disturbed, he debated whether to act upon the map or the native information; he decided to obey the letter of his instructions rather than his judgement and, still out of touch with his companion forces, moved forward to Chidane Meret proper. Now in full view of Adowa, he was fiercely attacked from all sides. Overwhelmed, outmanœuvred, and uncertain of his position, his plight was desperate. His native troops fought well, but could not hope to pierce their way back; finally they broke and ran; Albertone and the Italian officers were forced to surrender. The right wing, though better placed, was also cut off; their general killed, the troops fled back towards the centre body, spreading panic as they went. Some 8,000 Italians were killed outright, and some 4,000 of their native troops, while the fugitives who were not taken prisoners were harried in the narrow gorges which were their only way back to Eritrea. It is said that had Menelik not ordered all his troops back into camp on the evening of the battle, the cavalry could have cut off the few passes available and exterminated the whole Italian army.

The ignominy of this defeat was never forgotten in Italy. Writing to a young man bound for 'the African War' in 1935, the veteran Gabriele d'Annunzio urged him to wipe out its memory, for he could still feel on his shoulder 'the scar, yes, the shameful scar, of Adowa'.

The Italian Government was faced with making a humiliating peace in October 1896; they annulled the Treaty of Ucciali and recognized the full sovereignty and independence of Abyssinia. One thousand, eight hundred, and sixty-five prisoners were thereupon returned to Eritrea.

Stories of the barbarous mutilation inflicted upon these men are still current in Italy; actually thirty of the Italian prisoners returned to Rome mutilated according to the old Abyssinian custom, but this was contrary to Menelik's express order. The native Eritreans, who were viewed as traitors to their race, were less well treated, and 406 of them had their right hand and left foot cut off at his command. The Italians acknowledged Menelik's personal share in preventing the European captives from a like fate. The convention supplementary to the Peace Treaty stated that:

'The Italian plenipotentiary having spontaneously acknowledged that the prisoners have been the object of the greatest solicitude on the part of His Majesty the Emperor of Ethiopia, admits that their maintenance has entailed considerable expense, and that the Italian Government is indebted to His Majesty for sums corresponding to these expenses. His Majesty the Emperor of Ethiopia declares himself willing to leave it to the equity of the Italian Government to recompense him for these sacrifices.'

There is no public record of any further transaction, but the story of the well-being of the Italians is borne out by the British mission in 1897, who met released prisoners making their way down to the coast looking 'brown, healthy, and well-cared-for, and in tearing spirits at the idea of their speedy return to Europe'.

The victory over Italy placed Abyssinia on the map, and European delegations hurried to Addis Ababa—'New Flower'—which Menelik had built in 1883 to please his empress, and which was now the capital. The French were the first to arrive. The Governor of French Somaliland, travelling up into the Harar hills by mule caravan, was impressed by their amenities as compared with the coast; at Harar, Ras Makonnen received him with ceremony, and he went on to Addis Ababa in January 1897. Three months later Prince Henri d'Orléans, Duc de Valois, followed suit, bringing with him a handsome Sèvres china service for the emperor. Business representatives followed on his heels and so began the tortuous affair of the Jibuti railway over which British, French, and Italian representatives fought diplomatic battles for ten years. The French won, chiefly through the influence exercised on Menelik by his adviser, Monsieur Ilg—a Swiss engineer who had penetrated to Abyssinia nearly twenty years earlier in search of a career and whose top hat and frock coat, moustachios and spectacles were by 1897 an institution in Addis Ababa.

In July 1896 he had persuaded Menelik to hand over the railway concession of two years before to a French company, the *Compagnie internationale des Chemins de Fers Éthiopiens*. This built a section of the line from Jibuti towards Harar, and then ran out of funds. Recourse was had to British investors and the International Ethiopian Railway Trust was floated in London. This came to the ears of the French Colonial party, which waged a furious campaign against the employment of British capital in 'a purely French concern'. The French Government, anxious not to antagonize so loud-voiced a group, came to the railway's rescue, and in return for a 50-year subsidy took over virtual control of the line in 1902.

When Menelik learnt of this transaction he was not unnaturally incensed; it was unthinkable that a company which had had his gracious permission to operate should sell this right to a foreign government. He refused his permission to go on with the railway. The scheme stagnated for several years while the English and Italians struggled politely for the internationalization of the line, while the French representatives, with the Colonial party simmering in the background, stood the ground which Monsieur Ilg's favours had gained for them. No progress was made beyond Harar until the whole matter was settled by the agreement accompanying the Tripartite Treaty of 1906, when the French won the day so far as the line to Addis Ababa was concerned, and the British and Italians contented themselves with the right to build, beyond the capital, the lines which were to link it with their colonies to the north, south, and west—imaginary feats of engineering which have never materialized.

The French had no easy passage, and trains did not run through to Addis Ababa until 1918. Compensated by the dues they were able to levy on the goods carried on the line, they persevered in the face of obstruction after obstruction, bribing the Abyssinians with percentages on the cost of completing the unfinished sections and by other less mentionable means. Their reward is the high percentage of Abyssinian trade which passes through their port at Jibuti.

The British mission of 1897, under Mr. Rennell Rodd, followed so close in the tracks of the French that it caught up at Harar with some dilettante big-game-shooting members of Prince Henri d'Orléans' party. Menelik welcomed Mr. Rodd warmly, and seemed delighted with the polar bear skins, the silver-gilt jug and basin, and the gold-inlaid rifles which he brought him. He was particularly pleased with four silver-gilt rice-bowls: so much more useful, he pointed out, than the musical boxes and mechanical toys which were the usual stock-in trade of foreign visitors. Ras Makonnen, though friendly and a great admirer of England, which he visited in 1902, was more cautious: 'Les Anglais sont comme un chat qu'on caresse. Quand on le caresse, il est content; quand on veut l'enlever, il griffe.'

Caressing prevailed, and the mission departed with a treaty in its pack-saddles. This dealt with Somaliland problems only; it fixed the boundary, by inch-rule on a map,

1870–1916. THE EMPERORS VERSUS THE POWERS 149

and settled that the tribes on either side of it could move freely across it in their seasonal wanderings after pasture. The mission was agreeable and accommodating; it had crossed the line concerned, and saw little to be gained by claiming large tracts of the country: 'No villages enliven the route, and except for the numerous travellers that one meets going to and fro between Abyssinia and the sea, the only human beings to be seen are wandering Somalis pasturing their flocks or camels on the scrub and grass or watering them at the wells. To the uneducated eye there seems little nourishment for the camel in the dry thorns of the sunt tree (mimosa) or in the yellow and scanty patches from which the goats and sheep derive their sustenance; yet they seem to thrive on it.'[1] The green of the wooded Harar hills—'for by no stretch of imagination can one call the dust-coloured sunt tree really green'—looked like the Promised Land.

It was not until five years later, in 1902, that the British first secured rights in the real Land of Promise—the Lake Tsana region and the head waters of the Blue Nile, which the Abyssinians call the Abai. The river rises in the Gojjam highlands and enters the lake 6,000 feet above sea-level. For Europeans who can stand the altitude the climate is perfect. The point on which the attention of governments and engineers has for thirty years focused is that at which the Abai leaves the lake and plunges into the gorges of South Gojjam. A barrage here would be a reasonably simple feat of engineering, and the control of the waters means cotton and prosperity in Egypt and the Sudan; for it is the silt and mud deposits carried down from the Abyssinian highlands which each flood season fertilize the green belt which curls along the Nile's course through the plain. The Treaty of 1902 secured this flow to Egypt. The

[1] Lord Edward Gleichen, *With the Mission to Menelik*.

Abyssinians undertook not to allow any step which would divert the waters from their normal course to the Nile. There the matter rested; the French and Italians recognized the British rights in the region in the famous Tripartite Treaty of 1906, but no barrage was built, nor was much attention paid to the possibility of building one, until after the Great War.

Hard on the heels of the British mission came envoys from Turkey and the Czar; the Italians returned to the fray with commercial proposals and even the Dervishes sent an emissary. For the first time Addis Ababa teemed with foreigners. But beyond settling his boundaries with his three neighbours, which he did between 1897 and 1908, Menelik gave them little except a welcome. He let them concession after concession, some to scoundrels, some to stable concerns, some for coffee or cotton, some for the minerals existing in legendary quantities, some for skins and beeswax; one notorious hoax floated with British capital was a plan to grow rubber over several provinces. But the title deeds, at any rate on Menelik's side, were vague in the extreme; he let huge stretches of territory and pocketed the rent, but thought nothing of leasing an area to more than one concern at once; if the tribes shared their grazing grounds and agreed privately on their rights, why not the Europeans? The result was that few of the concessions survived the Great War; the notable exceptions were the French-run railway and the Bank of Abyssinia, which was established in 1905 under a concession to the National Bank of Egypt and still flourishes under the management of a cautious Scotsman, Mr. Collier. But even over these Menelik, as he grew older, grew more and more exacting; he imposed heavy percentages on the revenues of all foreigners and foreign companies; regardless of inconvenience, he forced all possible merchandise to pass through Addis Ababa simply in order to levy dues on it as it passed down to the railway; he also did a lucrative business as chief money-lender to the concessionaries at prohibitive rates of interest. He put little of this to commercial uses; spasmodically he built a road here and there, but except for the ever-lengthening French railway, means of communication remained poor, and in the rainy months —June to October—negligible. Practically the whole of his funds were spent on the army, which was excellent.

And well it needed to be so. Already in 1892–4 he had extended his domain by the conquest of the Wallamo lands north of Lake Abaya. From then until Adowa the Italians monopolized his time. In 1897 his generals Ras Gobana and Ras Makonnen marched west and conquered the Beni Shangul country overlooking the valley of the White Nile. Another army, farther south, subdued the rebel king of Kaffa and penetrated on towards Lake Rudolf. In 1898 expeditions set out under French influence, which was by now supreme in Addis Ababa. One, which was intended to join forces at Fashoda with Marchand, was actually officered, under an Abyssinian general, by a Frenchman, a Swiss, and a Russian. It reached the White Nile but not Fashoda, and was thus not involved in the famous Franco-British 'incident'. Yet another general, the famous old die-hard Fitaurari Hapta Giorgis, accompanied also by a Frenchman, marched south, to extend the empire as far as the desert of the Ogaden. Over this same Ogaden country, between 1900 and 1904, Abyssinian forces, at Menelik's suggestion, combined with the British to quell the activities of Mohammed Abdulla, known as the Mad Mullah, who for years spread sedition and rebellion among the Somalis in a vast tract of country running from British Somaliland to Harar, to the Haud in Italian Somaliland, and even farther south towards the British East African frontier. And sometimes, but not often, the imperial army was required to teach a lesson to some insurgent ras.

The leaders of these campaigns, and of a simultaneous series of scientific expeditions, also mainly sponsored by French explorers, brought map after map of unknown country back with them to Menelik. He at once claimed sovereignty over the places marked, by the simple expedient of affixing to the map the seal of the King of Kings.

To consolidate these acquisitions he needed their recognition by foreign powers, and between 1897 and 1908 he succeeded in negotiating a complete circle of boundary treaties with Great Britain, France, and Italy, demarcating Abyssinia as it is marked in any modern atlas. The one line over which there is doubt, since it was variously defined in the two treaties of 1897 and 1908 which cover it, is the frontier between Italian Somaliland and Abyssinia; uncertainty as to this was the cause of the trouble at Walwal which in December 1934 touched off the explosion with Italy.

Ever since his experience with the Italians over the protectorate clause in the Treaty of Ucciali, Menelik had been wary about his sovereign rights, and, jealous of his independence, had exercised extreme caution in every foreign deal. But from 1906 on his grip seemed to relax—a prelude to the stroke which almost completely paralysed him in 1908. In May 1906 it was rumoured that he had had an apoplectic fit. In the same spring, Ras Makonnen of Harar and Ras Mangasha of Tigré, the two most obvious successors to the throne, both died. Simultaneously, German influence began to grow at Addis Ababa. The three neighbour Powers grew anxious. In July 1906, without consulting Menelik, they concluded the famous Tripartite Treaty. They acknowledged Abyssinian independence, but 'in the event of rivalries or internal changes in Ethiopia' they recognized their mutual rights to take action to protect their nationals. They would not intervene, they agreed, in internal affairs, and 'in no case shall one of the three governments interfere in any manner whatsoever, except in agreement with the other two'. They then turned to the settlement of the vexed question of spheres of influence. While recognizing the validity of the agreements of the two previous decades (among them the Anglo-Italian agreement of 1891 which, they seemed to forget, recognized practically the whole of Abyssinia as an Italian sphere), they agreed, whatever happened, to concert to safeguard their respective interests in three loosely-defined areas: Great Britain in the Nile basin and round Lake Tsana, France round the railway, and Italy over a cresent-shaped strip between, linking Eritrea and Somaliland and running through the fertile highlands 'to the west of Addis Ababa'.

Menelik, when this came to his ears, was justly incensed. After long hesitation, which was unlike him and proves that his illness was already affecting him, he reluctantly accepted the situation on December 10, 1906:

'We have received the arrangement made by the three Powers. We thank them for their communication, and their desire to keep and maintain the independence of our Government. But let it be understood that this arrangement in no way limits what we consider our sovereign rights.'

For the next eighteen months, though partially paralysed, he still held the reins. In October 1907 he set up a ministry to assist him. In June of the next year he summoned the rases together and announced that he had appointed his grandson Lij Jasu, then a boy of twelve, to be his successor. In the autumn he was wholly paralysed, even as to speech, by a severe stroke. Apparently *in extremis*, he declared that Ras Tesamma was to be regent; he then sent for Lij Jasu and performed the solemn designation ceremony customary in Abyssinia. Committing the boy to the care of the abuna and the rases: 'Cursed shall he be', he said, 'who shall refuse to obey him, and he shall have a black dog for his son. If on his part he shall betray you in an unworthy manner, he himself shall be accursed, and he shall beget for his son a black dog.'

Menelik's grip once relaxed, all interested parties began to scheme and lobby for changes which might work out to their advantage. German influence was increasing at Addis Ababa; the empress had engaged a German governess for Lij Jasu and an Imperial Ethiopian Mission had been sent in the summer of 1907 to Berlin, Vienna, Budapest, Rome, and Constantinople. (The list is interesting, it being seven years before the World War.) To counteract this tendency towards Germanism, the vigorous French Minister-Plenipotentiary, Monsieur Klobukowski, wove a secret and competent network of exclusively French monopolies. He had arrived in Addis Ababa in the spring of 1907. By January 1908 he had achieved a new Treaty of Amity and Commerce, and a few weeks later he succeeded in inducing the ailing and reluctant Menelik to agree to the transfer of the old Jibuti railway concession to a new French company. At the same time he filled Addis Ababa with a host of French engineers, telegraphists, postal agents, agricultural experts, veterinary surgeons, and the like.

But the arch-schemers were the rases. The only deterrent to their activities was the fear that Menelik might regain his health and his faculties. As is often the way when a brain is numbed by disease in old age, he rallied from time to time, not markedly, but enough to instil an obvious wariness into the schemers.

The Empress Taitu did her best to step into the breach and to concentrate all political power in her hands. She was a shrewd woman of nearly sixty, vastly fat, but stately and very dignified, with a reputation for bravery gained by leading a regiment, in person, against some rebels in Tigré in 1902. She was Menelik's fourth wife, and he her fifth husband, and, with a varied experience behind her, she had always taken a leading part in the Emperor's counsels.

From the first she was anxious to get the rases to recognize Zauditu, the emperor's daughter by an earlier wife, as heir to the throne in place of Lij Jasu. She rightly recognized her as infinitely the more able of the two. But she did not play all her cards well; she made two bad mistakes. The first was when, foiled by the rases over the Zauditu issue, she invented a new post of 'adviser' to the emperor and filled it with a German, Dr. Zintgraff. Her enemies used every device to make his position untenable, and he resigned after a few months. The second was in her overanxiety to obtain the regency and the succession for her own family. She refused to acknowledge the merits of any but her blood relations, and even induced her nephew, Ras Gugsa, to sound the Sudan authorities as to their views about his accession to the throne.

By 1910 she had overreached herself. Matters came to a head when the abuna accused the supposed regent, Ras Tesamma, of having broken his oath to Menelik. The government took the necessary military measures and the empress, recognizing that she could do no more, surrendered unconditionally. There followed three years and more of complete disorganization; corruption and bribery were rife, and the slave trade increased. So did gun-running; indeed, the import of rifles reached such proportions that the British, French, and Italian legations, growing nervous, protested against the abuse of privileges secured to Abyssinia under the Brussels Act.[1] France even closed

---

[1] Signed in 1890 for control of the trade in arms and the slave trade in the interests of 'the preservation of the African populations'.

the port of Jibuti, but there were plenty of other open roadsteads on the coast. The trade continued, and anarchy flourished healthily all over the country.

These doings soon disposed of the thin veneer of modernity which Menelik's personal drive had imposed on Addis Ababa. In comparison with his great predecessors —Theodore, the noble savage who died of *folie de grandeur*, and John, a capable but harassed soldier—Menelik was a type belonging rather to the western business world, a pure-bred, hard-headed entrepreneur. He was keenly interested in foreign affairs, and his knowledge of the developments of European progress is commented on by almost every foreign visitor to his court. He even had advanced ideas about social reform, and decreed the abolition of slavery, the introduction of compulsory education, and the substitution of a new code for the old customary law. No doubt these would have been more effective had he personally supervised their execution; as it was, he was usually too busy consolidating his frontiers; few of his subjects grasped the significance of his ideas, and any benefits derived from the changes lapsed in the turbulent years of his illness and of Lij Jasu's short, eventful reign.

A few permanent marks of his modern mind survived the chaos. One is the postal system, with the stamps which bear his effigy; another, the electric light and telephone, which, advancing with the French railway, were installed in the palace at Addis Ababa as early as 1903. A third is the vaccination mark to be seen to-day on the skin even of elderly Abyssinians, for when cattle plague was rampant and small-pox ravaged the country in 1898 he ordered public prayer for deliverance but, as a further safeguard, issued an edict that all his subjects should be vaccinated. During his life, his mere name was a terror to evil-doers; since his death it has become a word on which to pledge an oath.

Lij Jasu was of a very different stamp, clever but dissolute and irresponsible. On the death of the regent, Ras Tesamma, in 1911, the Council had voted him old enough to act for himself under their guidance, and for the two years before Menelik's death he was in an invidious position, responsible but without power. This and the intrigues around him did his character no good; he strayed off with a small force into the Shankalla country towards the Nile plain and formed the first of a series of temporary 'betrothals' or 'marriages' (there is no exact English equivalent of the Amharic word) in the Moslem province of Gimirra. Here began the practices which were his downfall—the gradual adoption of the Moslem faith. Even before Menelik's death he antagonized the Shoan chiefs by his dalliance in the Moslem provinces. Next he attempted to dismiss some of the officers of importance still in attendance on the dying king, causing a palace skirmish, during which Taitu was obliged to have the paralysed emperor carried for safety to a cellar. Later a scandalized chronicler records how, in the week after Menelik died, he and his friends 'mounted their horses and rode away to enjoy themselves at picnics'.

Menelik's death on December 12, 1913, did not make much difference to the general turmoil. If anything it increased it, for the rases, freed of their fear of his recovery, began to fight among themselves for supremacy. In the early months of 1914 there was especial trouble in Tigré. Certain chiefs were attacked by their fellows and by the Government on the suspicion that they had received gifts from the Italians, whose designs on Abyssinia were feared at the time owing to the impression caused by their successes against the Turks in the Libyan war.

Abyssinia had the Great War to thank for a respite from foreign intervention during this turbulent period. The three interested Powers were fully occupied elsewhere. She, too, was wholly taken up with her own concerns—the intrigues among the rases and the great religious struggle with Lij Jasu—in relation to which the larger-scale struggle taking place beyond the frontiers was merely incidental.

Lij Jasu brought his predilections out into the open in 1915–16. He claimed that he was descended from Mohammed, not Solomon, and ordered the Moslem fakirs to produce a genealogy proving this. He wore the Moslem turban and scimitar, put away his Christian wife, and started a harem; he even negotiated with the Mad Mullah for marriage with his daughter. Finally, he presented the Turkish Consul-General with the green, red, and gold Abyssinian flag embroidered with a crescent and the device: 'There is no God but Allah.' He gave replicas to his Moslem subjects in the southern lowlands, and declared the country subject to the religious rule of Turkey.

Lij Jasu was not a force to be despised; he was shrewd, and in some ways far-sighted, and quick to deduce the factors in a situation which were capable of development to his advantage. This Turkish policy was not mere foolhardiness. Had it succeeded he would have created a Galla-Moslem backing which would have rendered him as powerful as any living ras.

Two groups in Addis Ababa viewed his doings with dismay. The first was the foreign legations. Both officially and privately, the British, Italian, and French representatives reasoned with him in an attempt to persuade him to abandon his tactics. They feared not so much the help that he could and did give to the Germans in East Africa as the possibility of a jihad, with a wholesale massacre of Christians and Jews which might have untold repercussions in important war areas. British, Italian, and

French troops were moved to Berbera, Massaua, and Jibuti respectively.

But the precaution proved needless, thanks to the activities of the second equally anxious faction in Abyssinia, the Shoan rases. In September 1916, Lij Jasu went down to Jigjiga in the southern lowlands to collect an army for his holy campaign. The Shoan chiefs at once massed their forces and marched into Addis Ababa. There they demanded of the abuna that he should release them from their oath of allegiance to Lij Jasu.

'We will never submit to Islam', runs their proclamation. 'We do not wish for our country to be delivered to the foreigner through the malice of Lij Jasu, who is leading our kingdom to ruin.' They declared Menelik's daughter Zauditu empress in his stead, with Ras Tafari, son of Ras Makonnen of Harar, as regent and heir to the throne. The abuna confirmed this and, through the Church, spread a message of loyalty and obedience to the new rule. Who failed in this would incur the wrath of the Father, the Son, and the Holy Ghost, of the Twelve Apostles and of the Three Hundred and Eighteen Fathers of the Council of Nicaea, the curse of Arius, and the reprobation of Judas. 'And', added the abuna, 'with my humble breath I excommunicate Lij Jasu.'

Thus admonished, the emperor fled from Harar into the country of the Danakils.

iii. 1916–1934. THE GROWTH OF A MODERN STATE

Zauditu was crowned on February 11, 1917. Next day Ras Woldo Giorgis was proclaimed Negus, for Ras Tafari, being only twenty-five, was thought too young for the honour.

The Negus must have been a dim personality, for he

counted for nothing in the intrigues which followed. The three leading figures at court, the empress, the regent, and the aged war minister, Fitaurari Hapta Giorgis, at once began to fence for position. Their three-cornered tussle continued for nearly ten years. They were almost equally matched in influence and following, and no one of them succeeded in gaining a marked advantage until death removed the Fitaurari in 1926.

Of the three, the regent had the hardest course to steer. He had inherited all Ras Makonnen's love of the modern and his desire for a westernized state. Fortunately for Abyssinia, Tafari's ideas were planted in a firm bedrock of common sense. He was also infinitely patient. He saw at once that it would be useless to try conclusions with the conservative factions round the throne, and contented himself with foreign contacts and with the slow but steady introduction of sensible innovations in the province of Harar, of which he was governor. Here he had opportunities for intercourse with the French, who were still busy on their railway, and whose language he spoke fluently. He visited the British at Aden in 1923, and, to the dismay of his retinue, made his first flight by aeroplane. In the same year he sent his wife Waizaro Manan to Egypt and Jerusalem. In 1925 he went to Europe, and when in England received back the Abyssinian crown which Napier had brought home as one of the few trophies of his success at Magdala.

The Fitaurari represented the opposite pole; he was old, irascible, fire-eating, and a confirmed die-hard. His long list of victories dated back to the days of Menelik. On the strength of them, he had an immense following among the older nobles, and led a group which preferred feudalism to a civil service, and deplored the newfangled notions which filled the head of young Ras Tafari.

The empress held on a middle course between the two, but, until the Fitaurari's death, joined forces with the enemies of change. At first her position was weak, and she tried to buttress it by the employment of a little-known German as adviser. This ranged the other two against her, and so she jettisoned the adviser, and contrived, in 1918, to rid herself of one menace by dissolving the Council of Ministers which dated from Menelik's illness. She now had to rely on her wits alone, on her prestige as a faithful and loving daughter to Menelik, and on her reputation for loyalty to those she trusted. In 1921 an unexpected trump card fell into her hands in the person of Lij Jasu.

For almost a year after his flight Lij Jasu had remained among the Danakils, while the northern provinces, uncertain whom to back, had risen and fought one another and the Government and proclaimed short-lived republics. Zauditu's fear was that he might go north and throw in his lot with the rebels; if so, she was not sure that she could count on the loyalty of her husband Ras Gugsa, in the north-west, of Ras Hailu, governor of Gojjam, or of Dejasmatch Balcha of Sidamo in the south. Her nervousness increased when Lij Jasu appeared in Magdala; then, for a breathing space, it was rumoured that he had died of fever. No one seemed sure; his existence was a sword of Damocles until his capture by government troops in 1921.

Even then she could not get rid of him by the usual means, for a decree of Menelik's ruled that no prince of the blood royal could suffer capital punishment. Instead she hit on a satisfying scheme; she would insure herself against an increase of power on the part of the dominant figures at court by entrusting his person to one of the other great rases, who could produce the puppet if need arose. It says much for the renown of young Ras Tafari that the Shoan chiefs extracted from her an oath not to send the captive to him at Harar. Trusting that the plan would not be turned to account against herself (a possibility which she realized but had to risk), she handed Lij Jasu over to Ras Kassa of Tigré, bound in the golden chains which befitted his royal rank.

The stalemate thus created ended with the death of the Fitaurari in 1926. The three-cornered struggle then turned into a straightforward tug-of-war, and the balance moved swiftly in favour of Ras Tafari. He was able to concentrate a large body of loyal troops more quickly than any of his rivals, and, with these behind him, to secure the dead man's governorships for himself and his nominees. The empress appealed to Ras Kassa, but Tafari was too quick for her and succeeded in obtaining the banishment of a leading trouble-maker, the etchegie, who as head of all the monastic orders was equal in influence to the abuna himself. Next he further consolidated his position by bringing Dejasmatch Balcha of Sidamo to book. The empress was powerless in face of this degree of control; in 1928 she gave her consent to his coronation as Negus.

Until this date, the only field in which his word had carried weight was that of foreign affairs. He had been told of the attention focused during the Versailles peace settlement on so-called humanitarian questions, among them the arms traffic and the slave trade, and he foresaw the possibility of outside interference on this score. Acting on the advice of foreign friends, he caused the Government in 1923 to send in a rather abrupt application for admission to the League of Nations.

The States Members discussed the question at length. Britain, Switzerland, Australia, and Norway were against immediate admission; they felt that more should be ascertained of the country's internal state, of the authority

1916–1934. THE GROWTH OF A MODERN STATE 163
of the central government and its capacity to prohibit the slave trade and to control the traffic in arms. France and Italy argued the contrary; League membership would strengthen the hand of the Government and so contribute to stamping out slavery, and promoting development. The Italian delegate pointed out that no special stipulations need be made to cover the import of arms, provided the powers supplied them to the Government only.

The Franco-Italian view prevailed. Subject to a declaration that, as regarded arms and ammunition, she would observe the St. Germain Arms Convention of 1919,[1] and that in this and all other matters she would 'furnish the Council with any information which it may require', Abyssinia was unanimously voted a League member on September 28, 1923.

This membership was soon to stand her in good stead.

Britain and Italy both had important interests in Abyssinia: the former, the water supply from Lake Tsana, the latter the rich 'sphere of influence' which had been designed, in 1906, to link Eritrea and Somaliland. Neither the World War nor the League of Nations drove these old treaties out of mind, and in 1919 the Italians proposed to the British Government that each should support the other in claiming concessions in the respective areas. The

[1] The international position as regards the arms trade needs a word of explanation. The St. Germain Convention for the Control of the Trade in Arms and Ammunition, signed by the Powers at the Peace Conference, never entered into force. The Geneva Convention for the Supervision of the Trade, signed in 1925, was designed to take its place, but failed to receive the number of ratifications necessary for validity. Abyssinia, who had adhered to both, was thus merely bound by the Brussels Act of 1890, which 'for the preservation of the African peoples' forbade the import of arms into a central part of Africa stretching from coast to coast. This position was hardly fitting for a sovereign League Member; hence the Arms Traffic Act signed in 1930 with Britain, France, and Italy, the three neighbour Powers.

British gain was to be a barrage on Lake Tsana and a motor road from the Sudan to the Lake; in return, they were to assist the Italians in obtaining a railway connecting Eritrea and Somaliland, running 'to the west of Addis Ababa', and a 'zone' along the length of the line.

But in 1919 the Italian Government was insecure and in bad odour at the Peace Conference, and the offer was not entertained. The British preferred to deal single-handed with an issue so vital as that of the Nile waters.

By 1925, the position had radically altered. The Fascist régime was firmly established and Signor Mussolini was well on the way to raising his country to the status of a great power. This time on British initiative, the same proposals were made; they were mutually agreed by an Exchange of Notes in December 1925. The British recognition of an Italian 'economic influence' in the railway zone was stipulated to be conditional upon obtaining the Tsana barrage concession and upon an Italian undertaking not to tamper with the Nile waterflow.

In accordance with the open procedure required of all League Members, the British and Italian notes effecting this transaction were duly published. Two interested parties were justly incensed. The French looked upon it as an infraction of the Tripartite Treaty of 1906, and a deal of explaining was required in Paris. The Abyssinians saw in it an intolerable affront to a fellow League Member. Upon hearing of it in June 1926, the regent forwarded notes of protest to both Italy and Great Britain. The former was a protest pure and simple, the latter more of a reproof: 'We should never have suspected that the British Government would come to an agreement with another Government regarding our Lake.'

He then referred the matter to the League of Nations. He succeeded in giving such publicity to the affair that no formal procedure was called for at Geneva. Both Powers hastened to explain away the phrasing of their notes. 'Italian economic influence', they said, merely meant freedom from competition as against British undertakings in the zone specified; of course the action of third parties, there as elsewhere in Abyssinia, was not and could not be limited by outside powers. Ras Tafari, having gained his point, let the whole matter drop. He merely stipulated that his protest should appear alongside the Notes in the published *Treaty Series* of the League of Nations. The whole incident is an illustration of the service the League machinery can render to a small state which has something to fear from a larger neighbour or neighbours.

Ras Tafari's rise to supreme power was at once reflected in the conduct of foreign policy. The westernization so dreaded by the Fitaurari's clique began without delay. The first step was the seeking of foreign help and advice.

In 1928 a twenty-year Treaty of Friendship was signed with Italy. Coming only two years after the brush over the Anglo-Italian transaction, this was at the time looked on as a diplomatic feat on the part of Signor Mussolini. But undoubtedly the two chief contributions to the agreement were to be found in Abyssinia: one was the tact and great understanding of the Abyssinians personified in the Italian Minister, Signor Giuliano Cora; the other was Ras Tafari's determination to open up the country. In an accompanying convention he secured an Abyssinian free zone at the Italian port of Assab. A motor road was to connect this with the town of Dessieh in north-east Abyssinia, each party building the section in its own territory, and an Italo-Abyssinian company was to have the monopoly of the road traffic. The advantages to both sides were obvious.

Ras Tafari then turned to the army. In 1929 he engaged

166 1916–1934. THE GROWTH OF A MODERN STATE

a Belgian military mission to train a royal bodyguard. He intended thus to familiarize a nucleus with modern methods and modern weapons.

1930 was a busy year. He embarked upon negotiations for a state bank. Next, after consultation with the Sudan Government over the Lake Tsana question, he sought tenders for building the long-envisaged barrage, and instructed an American firm, the J. G. White Engineering Corporation, to survey the lake. Progress was well on the way when the cotton crisis broke on the world, and for the time being put expenditure on the project out of the question.[1]

Church matters, too, received attention. He secured the appointment of a new Coptic abuna, Monsignor Kyril, and the consecration of five Abyssinian bishops. He even persuaded the Patriarch of Alexandria to brave the journey and visit his daughter church.

In August he regularized the arms position by the signature of the Arms Traffic Act with Britain, France, and Italy. This, while preventing the import of arms for unauthorized persons, enabled him 'to obtain all the arms and munitions necessary for the defence of his territories from external aggression and for the preservation of internal order therein'.

Home politics could not be conducted at this pace. As well he knew, there must be no sweeping changes; the new must be grafted little by little on to the old. Even if he had lacked the wisdom to see this, unrest in the provinces would have prevented progress. So long as the

[1] It was revived by the Abyssinian Government in a proposal to the British, Egyptian, and Sudan Governments in May 1935, but these refused to take any step which might aggravate the dispute with Italy, then in full course. Nevertheless the Egyptian Government, in its 1935 Public Works project, voted £E21 millions towards building the barrage.

empress lived and the power remained divided, even nominally, in Addis Ababa, the respect of the rases for authority was divided also. They were still a force to be reckoned with.

He was too prompt for them in the so-called Palace Revolt of 1928, and the day of reckoning did not come until March 1930. Ras Gugsa, Zauditu's husband, rebelled in the north, where he had been spreading sedition for some time. For days the townspeople of Addis Ababa were uncertain what was happening. Troops were moving north, but no one knew where; it was rumoured that Ras Kassa of Tigré and Ras Hailu of Gojjam had joined the rebels. The town awoke some days later to the first definite news: a *coup* for Ras Tafari. He had ringed round the rebels with his loyal troops, and from two aeroplanes had bombed them with pamphlets. One, from the abuna, declared that Ras Tafari was a true son of the Church. This quelled the spirit of rebellion, and the victory of the Negus was complete.

The brief interlude during which his power was absolute in all but name lasted for only two days, for the Empress Zauditu died on April 2, 1930. His coronation as emperor followed on November 2, when, founding a new dynasty, he took the throne-name Haile Selassie I.

Arrays of princes and powers attended the ceremony, at which Great Britain was represented by the Duke of Gloucester. The British royal suite included members of the diplomatic corps and a naval detachment, and was followed by a retinue of journalists and one satiric novelist; there is thus no dearth of description of the scene. The colours were magnificent as ras after ras in full regalia bowed in homage before the imperial throne. The newly trained bodyguard put up a good display and, thanks to a little road repair, even the rather haphazard lay-out of

Addis Ababa managed to look quite imposing. The residents scoffed at the window-dressing, but the visitors appreciated the effort.

Haile Selassie was now free to start his new deal. His natural patience and caution had increased in the fourteen difficult years during which he had bided his time. Wisely, he did not attempt to go too fast. He avoided the fatal mistake which King Amanullah had made in Afghanistan. This gained him a valuable backing among the older men. His caution was galling to young Abyssinia—to the *intelligentzia* who had been to Europe, twenty of them at his personal expense—but this left wing was to act rather as a spur than as a revolutionary element.

The mainspring of his scheme was the creation of a loyal state, secure against sedition and, therefore, against dismemberment or aggression. This achieved, westernization would in time automatically follow. By far his most important reform, therefore, was the gradual appointment to the governorships of the various provinces of trusted friends of his own. Wherever possible, he put in a man with European experience; one had been minister in Paris, another in Rome, a third was a doctor with long experience in India, and so forth. Since the Abyssinians are a people accustomed to act with complete faith upon the word of their chief, the significance of this change is capital.

In 1932 he achieved a great step in the desired direction when Ras Hailu of Gojjam rebelled in support of Lij Jasu's last bid for liberty and power. The Government troops put down the insurrection and, with a new governor, Gojjam also was drawn into the loyal fold. Kassa of Tigré was the only powerful member of the old school of highland rases to remain supreme.

Compared in importance with this fundamental change,

almost all the other innovations which Haile Selassie has introduced are so far slight. They make a showing in Addis Ababa, and for a few miles round the town, but elsewhere they as yet count for nothing.

His first such inauguration was the constitution which he granted on July 16, 1931. He explained to an assembly of princes, rases, chiefs, and church dignitaries that for long years it had been necessary for him to govern like a father, guiding his people in the way they should go. Now the nation was making great strides forward and the time had come for his people to share the task which hitherto he had performed alone.

The Parliament 'designated by the provinces subject to our consent' met periodically, and discussed the new company, currency, and bankruptcy laws and dealt with regulation of the holding of property by foreigners, but in fact its proceedings were a matter of form and Haile Selassie continued to govern single-handed. Its important contribution to development was the use the emperor made of it to spread a knowledge of modern administrative machinery. In order that the little leaven might leaven the whole lump he changed the local representatives in both Senate and Chamber every three months. He also created three model provinces with a governor and civil service appointed by the central Government.

He engaged further foreign advisers in order to speed achievement. The Belgians already at work on the army were joined by Swedish officers and by a Swiss bandmaster. Another Belgian mission was employed to train the police.

An effort was made to render education compulsory for all children and further schools were set up, but outside the capital this rule remained a dead letter.

In co-operation with certain of the diplomatic corps,

the emperor also set about improving the smooth working of justice. Under the present rather haphazard system, cases of minor importance can be heard in the street before any arbiter chosen on the spot; plaintiff and defendant can have out their difference in front of the policeman on point duty. Only major cases go to the expense of the courts, important cases to the Supreme Court presided over by the emperor himself. An eye for an eye is the prevailing standard; debtors go chained to their creditors till the debt is paid, and legal awards are apt to leave justice to be done by the family of the plaintiff. Foreigners, or any one who can claim the protection of a foreign consulate, are entitled to be tried in a court in which their consul sits as a member. The British consuls have their hands full with cases involving the many British-Indian and British-Somali traders in the country.

Of the new measures of Haile Selassie's first four years, those taken against slavery attracted the most attention in the world outside. The custom, which is time-old in Abyssinia, was abolished by the Emperor John and again by the Emperor Menelik, but their decrees were purely formal. The practice persisted. In the disturbed years of Menelik's illness and the reign of Lij Jasu it flourished and increased; the Empress Zauditu and her regent had therefore to make a completely new start when they began to try to fulfil the state's obligations as a member of the League of Nations. The first of their abolition laws was passed in 1924, and in 1931 Haile Selassie followed it up with a rather more radical decree. Between them, these laws promised in time to improve matters as they emancipated children born to slave parents, and slaves on their owners' deaths, but they proved hard to put into effect. A major difficulty was that even high officials continued to be concerned in the enslaving of new servants.

In 1932 Lord Noel Buxton visited the emperor on behalf of the Anti-Slavery and Aborigines Protection Society and secured from him a promise to bring the custom to an end within twenty years. As good as his word, Haile Selassie forthwith set up a Slavery Bureau in Addis Ababa, under the management of an English adviser. By 1934 he was able to report the establishment of sixty-two local bureaux, to which he had attached judges responsible for the freeing of slaves and for punishment of offences under the laws. The effort, therefore, was considerable, but the immediate results were negligible. Even the young generation of well-to-do westernized Abyssinians, though opposed to the custom, feel that the Government cannot go too slowly in the matter of abolition. They point out that a sudden forcible change would cause an economic upheaval which would fall heaviest on the heads of the liberated slaves, men and women who have never been accustomed to fend for themselves. They point out, too, that the greatest evil lies not in domestic slavery, but in the international traffic to Arabia, which is necessarily carried on through the European colonies on the coast. They rightly argue that this is the head at which first to strike.

Haile Selassie's task has not been easy. The chief element with which he has had to contend is the conservatism of the older generation. As all over the Orient, the respect for old age in Abyssinia is enormous. Grey hairs denote wisdom, and in order to promote confidence the emperor is obliged to choose as his advisers and members of Parliament men whose instincts are averse to change.

Nevertheless he has made progress. Commercially the change is insignificant, and will continue so until better means of communication are established. Apart from the railway there are only two good routes, the lorry road from Berbera in British Somaliland via Hargeisha to Harar, and the road south from Addis Ababa towards Jimma and Kaffa, also possible for motor traffic. To the west, the trade route via Gambela in the Sudan is a mule route only, and the two roads north from Addis Ababa, one towards Lake Tsana and one towards Tigré, are impassable in the rainy season. Without roads, development cannot proceed beyond Addis Ababa.

At the same time the world crisis has not helped matters. Abyssinia is practically self-supporting, and has therefore suffered less than many other parts of Africa, but her currency has fallen seriously in value. The thaler, which was worth three or four to the pound sterling before the war, by 1929 stood at 12, and by 1931 at over 20; it has since continued to fall. This had a pronounced effect upon the import trade, for the Abyssinian prefers to do without a luxury rather than to pay for it at double its old price. A result of the situation has been to place practically the whole import trade of textiles into Japanese hands, cheap goods only being saleable. The export trade suffered in relation to the falling off of imports, and its difficulties were aggravated by the immensely high freight rates on the railway, which average £43 per ton. (For purposes of comparison the English figure, in similar conditions, is £4.) Nevertheless, Jibuti continues to be the chief channel for foreign traffic, carrying about 65 per cent. of the total, the remainder going some 20 per cent. through the Sudan, 10 per cent. through Eritrea, and 5 per cent. through British Somaliland.

The field in which progress is really marked is in the unification of the empire. Provinces with western-trained governors can, for almost the first time, be relied upon to respond with loyalty to orders from the present administration. By 1934, these provinces extended over the whole of Shoa, Amhara, and Gojjam, and in certain of the southern districts such as Sidamo and Kaffa, towards the frontiers of Kenya. Ras Kassa of Tigré in the north, as belonging to the old régime, was a less certain quantity. So was the quasi-autonomous Sultan of Jimma, but these, being before all things Abyssinians, were thought likely to rally to the emperor's summons in the event of a threat from abroad.

Less well in hand are the wild tribes of the frontier areas who have scarcely heard of the new ruler. The late Mr. L. M. Nesbitt, exploring in the Aussa and Danakil country, wrote of the former tribe that the sole tie existing between them and the capital was 'the artful, or foolish, council chamber convention by which the Aussa falls within the boundary of the Ethiopian Empire. So it is marked on maps, things of the existence of which the Aussans are sublimely ignorant.'[1] The same is true of the Danakils, in whose country his chief impressions were 'the laughter of hyenas, the shrieks of monkeys, the blowing and snorting of hippopotami, and the roaring, splashing, and thudding of fighting crocodiles'. The Ogaden—the chief Somali tribe of the south—are equally primitive and lacking in consciousness of the nation to which, officially, they belong. It is thought by foreign observers that they would tend to resist a European invader, but that they would be as likely to harry both sides, with a view to loot, as actively to assist the Abyssinians proper. Whatever the progress made in Addis Ababa, it will for years to come be idle to mention the word modernization in the same breath as these wild lowland tribes. It is they who, bent on blood feuds and quarrels over wells and grazing grounds, are responsible for the frequent raids into British, French, and

[1] *Desert and Forest.* Cape, 1934.

Italian territory. The modern frontier lines are as little known to them as is a national feeling for Abyssinia.

Faced with the threat of aggression and the prospect of national defence two great unifying factors were the army and the Church. Antagonisms between the Christian highlanders and the Moslem Gallas and lowlanders (the Danakils and Aussans and the Somalis of the Ogaden all profess forms of the Moslem faith) vanished before the common danger, and united religious demonstrations were frequent in the streets of the capital. The only districts unlinked by this new bond were the pagan provinces of the south-west and extreme west.

Recruiting, too, threw together sects and races who would normally have no intercourse. Cushites, the dominant race, were to be seen drilling beside Falasha Jews, Gallas, and Somalis. Postal clerks, railway employees, and Guragis, the servant race, for the first time rubbed shoulders with up-country peasants whose only training was *watarane*, the two months' service given to their chief each year in return for the land they till. The spirit was willing; the weakness was the lack of equipment for war with a modern mechanized power. The discrepancy was far greater in 1935 than at Magdala in 1868 or Adowa in 1896, and was heightened by the arms embargo on both disputants declared in July 1935 by all the great arms-manufacturing countries except Japan.

Abyssinia's chief defence therefore remained her mountains. The will to defend them against an invader constituted a great national binding force. In a few months it did more to unify the state than could Haile Selassie have achieved over years of leisurely prosperity.

PART VI

1934–1935. THE DISPUTE WITH ITALY

THE story of Abyssinia's relations with Italy following the 1928 Treaty of Friendship demands a chapter apart. Writing at the height of the dispute, it would be impossible to deal with it without undue bias in the course of a history of independent Abyssinia. Moreover, there are two versions, usually contradictory, to every incident since the Treaty, and for the time being neither can be checked with reliability.

An instance of this kind of discrepancy arises over the convention supplementary to the Treaty, whereby Abyssinia was to acquire a free zone at the Italian port of Assab, to be reached by a motor road jointly built and jointly controlled. The Abyssinians held that it proved impossible to carry out the first part of the project—the road-building —because the Italians, given an inch in Abyssinian territory, from the outset tried to seize an ell. The Italian account was that whereas the Eritrean sector of the road was built with success, the Abyssinians, in their sector, consulted Dutch engineers wholly unused to the type of road-building required, and refused to employ the experienced Italians available. The result was that the Abyssinian plans produced were quite impracticable. More than this, the Abyssinian Government put a stop to all progress by issuing a decree that no roads should be built unless linked with Addis Ababa. (Dessieh, the terminus of the projected Italo-Abyssinian road, was linked by a track only.) The Italians added that in spite of this decree a road unlinked with the capital was built from Harar province towards British Somaliland.

Contradictions of this kind abound.

1934–1935. THE DISPUTE WITH ITALY

The ill feeling which exploded at Walwal on December 5, 1934, had thus been simmering for some time. The Italians, in an immense dossier which they did not produce until the quarrel had reached its height in September 1935, quoted instance after instance of Abyssinian 'raids, aggressions, and attempted invasions' on their frontiers, but many of the cases given were of the type with which the British and French frontier authorities are familiar, and handle, as purely tribal feuds, with a subaltern and a few native troops. All three of the neighbour powers experienced this type of raiding during 1932–3. It was at one time so prevalent on the French Somaliland frontier that 200 Senegalese and some military aeroplanes were dispatched to Jibuti, but despite precautions a French commissioner was murdered when a Danakil tribe raided the neighbouring Eisa, across the frontier, in January 1935.

The stages by which the Italian government came to look on these activities as 'rabid Abyssinian xenophobia' and as a threat to Italy's African colonies are hard to determine.

Clearly, feeling was running high early in 1934, and the Italians subsequently asserted that by July Abyssinian irregulars, under one Omar Samantar, an Italian deserter with a price on his head, were massing near their Somaliland frontier. It is therefore rather surprising that the Italian Government agreed to reaffirm the 1928 Treaty of Friendship in a declaration issued in Rome on September 29, 1934.

In November a minor clash occurred when some Abyssinian rowdies attacked the Italian consulate at Gondar, but the Abyssinian Government immediately paid the full reparation demanded.

The far-reaching Walwal incident arose in connexion with the operations of an Anglo-Abyssinian Boundary

1934–1935. THE DISPUTE WITH ITALY

Commission which had been demarcating the frontier between Abyssinia and British Somaliland, and had been instructed to survey the wells and watering grounds shared by certain British-Somali tribes and the Abyssinian Ogaden. The Italo-Abyssinian boundary in this region, though loosely (and conflictingly) defined in two treaties dating back to Menelik's day, had never been demarcated on the spot, but, according to the interpretation most favourable to the Italians, ran at a distance of 180 miles from the coast. The important wells of Walwal and Wardair, which lie over 230 miles inland, were in 1930 occupied by the Italian Somaliland authorities, who built fortified posts near the water. This occupation never occasioned a protest from Addis Ababa, and the Italian authorities were convinced that the area was recognized as being under their authority both by the Abyssinians and the British, whose tribes used the wells.

They were wrong in this assumption, for the Joint Anglo-Abyssinian Commission visited the wells on November 23, 1934, as being in Abyssinian territory.

A protective escort of about 600 regular and irregular Abyssinian troops accompanied the Commission. Difficulties at once arose over the question of access to the water. The British officers on the Commission reported the Italian commander to be 'unconciliatory and disobliging', and, when Italian military aeroplanes gave a 'provocative demonstration' over the camp, they decided to play for safety and withdraw. The Italians later explained that they had merely been taking air photographs.

The Joint Commission therefore left the wells, but in order to avoid any appearance of a retreat, which might have roused the Ogaden, and have amounted to an acknowledgement of Italian possession, left a force on the spot.

Excitement and suspicion prevailed in both camps. The ingredients for a clash were all to hand. A pitched battle took place on December 5, 1934. No neutral eyewitness was present, and it is impossible to lay the whole responsibility at either door; this, at any rate, was the ultimate decision reached by the Commission of Enquiry into the matter.

Each party indicted the other. Italy at once demanded apologies, a salute to the Italian flag at Walwal, and £20,000 compensation, but the Abyssinians refused until the blame had been fairly assigned. Since Italy refused arbitration, the Abyssinian Government referred the matter to the League of Nations.

For some months the dispute did not assume threatening dimensions. Owing, no doubt, to anxiety to settle it as unobtrusively as possible, it was not discussed by the League Council meeting of January 1935, nor at the meeting of the British, French, and Italian premiers at Stresa in the following April. This silence later proved to have been a great mistake, for the Italian Government took it to mean that the European powers would turn a blind eye to their doings in Africa. This impression was heightened by an agreement which they signed with the French on January 7, 1935, establishing a joint front in Europe and adjusting certain territorial claims in Africa owed by France to Italy since the Great War. By one clause, France handed over to Italy 2,500 out of her 34,000 shares in the Jibuti–Addis Ababa railway. A further secret clause referred to Abyssinia in ambiguous terms which the French interpreted as a warning, the Italians as an intimation that they might go ahead.

In February the Italians began to take military precautions and to send troops and Blackshirts to East Africa, but both parties seemed ready to negotiate, and the prospects of peaceful settlement still looked fair. In May 1935 the League Council dealt with the question and succeeded in setting on foot the arbitral procedure provided for in the article of the 1928 Treaty of Friendship, by which both parties undertook not to resort to force. An arbitration commission of four—two Italians and two lawyers, a Frenchman and an American, employed by Abyssinia—was to discuss the matter. If it had not reached agreement, or appointed a fifth neutral arbitrator, by July 25 the Council was to meet again. Failing a final settlement by August 25 the Council would meet in any case.

The tempo began to quicken. Military preparations increased in Italy and patriotic headlines sprang out in the Italian press.

The Conciliation Commission failed to agree. The Italians would not hear of a fifth arbitrator; the Abyssinians wished to discuss the whole question of frontier rights and not simply the responsibility for Walwal. The deadlock was complete and the League Council therefore met again at the end of July 1935. It succeeded in setting the Commission back to work with a fifth arbitrator—a point to Abyssinia, but with terms of reference strictly confined to Walwal—a point to Italy. It also resolved that:

'The Council decides to meet in any event on September 4 to undertake the general examination in its various aspects of the relations between Italy and Ethiopia.'

The Italians abstained from voting on this resolution.

Meantime a solution was sought in a separate Three-Power meeting of the signatories of the 1906 Tripartite Agreement. The British, French, and Italians met in Paris on August 16, 1935. From here, the British and French delegations forwarded to Rome proposals to which the consent of Abyssinia could be secured. The offer was comprehensive, and most advantageous to Italy. It covered development and reorganization with the collective assistance of the three powers over all fields of Abyssinian national life: economic, financial, commercial, constructional, foreign concessions and settlement, modernization of the administration, anti-slavery measures, and police services. It suggested 'particular account being taken of the special interests of Italy';[1] it did not exclude the possibility of territorial adjustments. The one proviso was that these reforms should be freely assented to by Abyssinia in the fullness of her sovereignty.

But by this time the desire for possession was burning too high in Italy. The answer was a blank refusal. It was logical and honest that the Italian delegate at the League Council meeting of September 4, 1935, should make what was, in all but name, a declaration of war. Abyssinian policy, he said, had forced Italy to the conclusion that she had to do with a permanent enemy; all possibility of peaceful collaboration had failed, and it was now beneath the dignity of the Italian Government to treat with Abyssinia on a footing of equality before the tribunal of the League of Nations.

From now on, the Italian cards were all on the table.

The mental process by which the Italian Government reached this stage is hard to follow. The press is no guide, for, being subject to censor, it loud- and soft-pedalled the news in accordance with day to day orders from headquarters. The resulting changes of tone deceived no one abroad.

Certainly the idea of immediate large-scale aggrandizement at Abyssinia's expense germinated sometime in 1935. Only on March 18, 1934, Signor Mussolini had announced to the Quinquennial Assembly of Fascists that 'there must be no misunderstanding upon this centuries-old task which

[1] Mr. Eden to the League Council, September 4, 1935.

I assign to this and future generations of Italians. There is no question of territorial conquests—this must be understood by all both far and near—but of a natural expansion which ought to lead to a collaboration between Italy and the peoples of Africa, between Italy and the nations of the Near and Middle East.'

But the jingoism which inevitably accompanies mobilization and the dispatch of troopships changed this tone. By May 24, 1935, it had become: 'Let no one hold any illusions in or out of Italy. We are tolerably circumspect before we make a decision, but once a decision is taken we march ahead and do not turn back.' By July 31 all motives such as the abolition of slavery and the advancement of civilization had been discarded as irrelevant, and the essential arguments were two: the vital needs of the Italian people and their security in East Africa; 'any action of expansion or any protectorate must be accompanied by military measures'. By August 18: 'We must go forward until we achieve the Fascist Empire.'

No reasonable person can quarrel with the case for Italian expansion; it is excellent, and pressing. Italy is a virile nation needing raw materials for her growing industries and an outlet for her surplus population. She came too late into the nineteenth-century scramble for colonies, and, owing to an inefficient government, was poorly treated at the Peace Conference. Adjustments are clearly called for.

Unfortunately, she played her hand badly. By her behaviour over the Abyssinian dispute she antagonized world opinion and so infinitely weakened her case.

She baffled those who tried to understand her by perpetually shifting the grounds on which she based her action. They ranged from assistance to a backward people, to the advancement of civilization, the prevention of Japanese expansion,[1] her own need for outlets, and the conquest of a Fascist empire; even her most faithful supporters were sometimes uncertain which tune to sing. Added to this was a haughty unwillingness to set out her case. She did not think fit to produce the enormous dossier indicting Abyssinia as unfit for independent status until September 1935, that is, *after* she had ranged world opinion against herself by turning down advantageous offers of peaceful settlement, and by making mass preparation for war against a lesser neighbour. She argued that she was merely doing what others had done in the last century, but this was a bad miscalculation of post-war world standards. To the dismay of all her friends, her handling of the international side of the dispute could hardly have been more clumsy. Even when she had decided to stake everything on conquest, her very honesty was unsubtle; she would have been far harder to contend with had she done as Japan did over Manchukuo in 1931-1932—played for delay by paying lip-service to peaceful means at Geneva, but gone quietly forward in Africa.

There were many good points in the Italian case against Abyssinia, but their effect on public opinion was neutralized by these psychological mistakes. Slavery, the wild conditions on the frontiers, the barbaric mutilations which were still the punishment for crime, the cruelty of many native customs, the lack of imperial control over outlying provinces, the primitive state of national development—all tended to be forgotten in the wave of world sympathy evoked by the tactics of the Italian Government.

Abyssinia thus acquired almost world-wide moral support. The Emperor Haile Selassie further strengthened

---

[1] Japan is the principal source of Abyssinian imports, and in 1934 it was falsely rumoured that she had been granted vast cotton-growing concessions.

her case by the dignity with which he handled the situation, and by the calm and moderation which he successfully instilled into all his people during the most difficult months of the dispute. There could have been no better proof of the degree of control he had established throughout the country.

But if the nation were forced to defend her independence against an invader, he knew her chief strength to be her time-old ally, the nature of her territory:

'If the efforts of other nations and our own fail, and devilish violence takes the opportunity to begin war, sowing misfortune, shame, and misery with the world as its field, Ethiopia will rise up, the Emperor at her head, and follow him in her hundred thousands with the valour and staunchness famous for a thousand years. Leaning on the Divine arm, she will resist the invader to her last drop of blood, fighting from the natural fortresses of mountain and desert that the Lord has given her.'

INDEX

Abai (Blue Nile), 2, 3, 25, 48, 104, 123, 127, 149.
Abraha, King, 29, 30, 72.
Abu Salih, 19, 61.
Abuna, the, 36, 47–8, 50–2, 68, 75–6, 86–7, 88–90, 94–6, 110, 121, 124, 129, 155, 159, 166–7.
Addis Ababa, 1–2, 9, 146–8, 150–1, 153–4, 156, 158–9, 164, 167–73, 175, 177–8.
Adel, 55–6, 82, 90–1, 105.
Adowa, 139, 144–5.
Adulis, 22–4, 30, 34, 46.
Aeizanas, King, 24–5, 28, 30.
Agaus, the, 8–9, 31, 40, 42, 48–9, 94.
Ahmed Gran, 82–5, 87, 90, 102, 106, 108.
Albuquerque, 3, 62.
Alexander, King, 55, 69.
Alexandria, the patriarch of, 3, 19–20, 27–8, 35–8, 47–8, 50–3, 57, 66, 88, 166.
Ali, Ras, 128–9.
Alvarez, Francisco, 58, 62 seqq., 81, 102.
Amba Geshen, 72, 83.
Amba Wahni, 72, 108, 110, 123.
'Amda Seyon, King, 3, 55, 80.
Amhara, 8–9, 46, 66, 80, 122, 126, 128, 130, 173.
Angot, 66, 80.
Aphilas, King, 24, 34.
Ark of the Covenant, the, 14, 15, 19–21, 74.
Army, the, 64–5, 126, 165–6, 169, 174.
Assab, 137, 165, 175.
Athanasius, 27–8, 35–7.
Atsbeha, *see* Ellesbaas.
Aussans, the, 173–4.
Axum, 7, 9, 16, 18, 20, 22–4, 28, 30–1, 33, 35, 67, 74, 91, 106, 108, 114, 144.

Ba'eda Maryam, King, 55, 72, 80.
Bahrmedr, Bahrnagas, 64–6, 80, 83, 90–1, 99.

Bakaffa, 118–20.
Bali, 55, 85.
Baratieri, General, 143–4.
Barreto, Patriarch John Nunez, 88, 91.
Basilides, King, 72, 97–100, 108–9, 125.
Begamedr, 67, 80, 106, 122–3, 126.
Bejas, the, 9, 23–5, 46, 124.
Bell, John, 129–31.
Berbera, 135, 139, 172.
Bermudez, John, 83, 85–9.
Blue Nile, *see* Abai.
Brancaleone, Nicholas, 58, 76.
Britain, relations to Abyssinia, 127, 129–34, 136, 141–2, 148–9, 152–3, 158, 162–4.
Bruce, James, 43, 72, 101, 110, 114–15, 119 note, 120, 123–7, 135.

Cameron, Captain, 132.
Candace, Queen, 29.
Ceremonies of the court, 32–3, 68–9, 106–7, 124–5.
Church, Abyssinian, foundation of, 26 seqq.; customs of, 38 seqq., 52, 57, 73–6, 89–90; constitution of, 33–6, 49–52, 111, 167; doctrines of, 36–8, 57, 109–10.
Claudius, King, 83–90, 98.
Covilham, Peter de, 62, 66, 76, 79.

Dahlak, 46, 48.
Dambya, 67, 80, 105, 106.
Damot, 48, 67, 104, 122–3.
Danakil, 1, 2, 7, 23, 84, 96, 103, 130, 159, 161, 173–4, 176.
David, King, 118; *see also* Lebna Dengel.
Debaroa, 83–4, 90.
Debra Damo, 72.
Debra Libanos, 97, 109, 118.
Dessieh, 165, 175.
Doaro, 55, 63, 85, 87.

INDEX

Ella Amida, King, 24, 28, 34.
Ellesbaas (Ella Atsbeha, Kaleb), King, 16, 29, 30, 32, 34, 42, 44.
Enarya, 91, 104, 106.
Eritrea, 9, 137 seqq., 140, 145–6, 153, 163–4, 172, 175.
Ethiopia, Abyssinia so called, 10, 16–17, 24 note.

Falashas, the, 40 seqq., 91, 95, 174.
Fashoda, 151.
Fasil, 122–3, 126.
Fatigar, 55, 66, 80, 85.
Florence, Council of, 57.
France, relations to Abyssinia, 111 seqq., 136, 141–2, 146–8, 152–3, 158, 163–4.
Fremona, 91–3, 98.
Frumentius, 26–9, 34–7, 42.

Gafat, 67, 80.
Gallas, the, 8–10, 58, 63, 85, 87, 91, 94–5, 97, 102, 104–6, 108, 118–19, 122–3, 126, 130–1, 136, 141, 143, 158, 174.
Gama, Vasco da, 62, 83; Christopher da, 83–4, 86.
Gimirra, 157.
Gingiro, 104–5.
Gojjam, 3, 8–9, 64, 67, 80, 95, 106, 128, 130, 143, 149, 161, 167–8, 173.
Gondar, 9, 108, 112–13, 118–19, 121–3, 125–30, 176.
Goragé, 66.
Guardafui, Cape, 62, 140.
Gugsa, Ras, 155, 161, 167.
Guragis, the, 174.

Hadya, 55, 63, 80.
Haile Selassie, King, *see* Tafari, Ras.
Hailu, Ras, 161, 167–8.
Hapta Giorgis, Fitarauri, 151, 160–2, 165.
Harar, 1, 135–6, 139–41, 143, 146–9, 159–60, 162, 172, 175.
Hawash, River, 2.
Hejjaz, 23, 41–2, 81.
Helena, Queen, 62–4.

Ismail, Khedive, 135.
Italy, relations to Abyssinia, 136 seqq., 152–3, 158, 163–5, 175 seqq.

Jacob, King, 93.
Jesuits, 88, 111 seqq.
Jesus I, King, 110–12, 115, 117–18, 120.
Jesus II, King, 120–2, 125.
Jibuti, 2, 142, 144, 147–8, 154, 159, 172, 176, 178.
Jimma, 172–3.
Joas, King, 122–3.
John I, King, 108–9.
John II, King, 123.
John III, King, 130, 134.
John IV, King, 20, 134–8, 156, 170.
Juba, River, 2, 140.
Justice, administration of, 69 seqq., 125, 170.
Justinian, Emperor, 32, 38, 44.
Justus, King, 117–18.

Kaffa, 6, 8, 91, 104, 136, 151, 172.
Kaleb, *see* Ellesbaas.
Kassa, Ras, 162, 167–8, 173.
Kebra Nagast, the, 18–20, 30, 54.

Lalibala, King, 49, 54.
Lasta, 49.
League of Nations, the, 162–5, 170, 178–80.
Lebna Dengel (David), King, 55, 62–3, 79, 83, 86, 88–9, 139.
Lij Jasu, King, 153–4, 156–9, 161–2, 168, 170.
Literature, Abyssinian, 34–5, 53–5.

Mad Mullah, the, 140, 151, 158.
Magdala, 130, 132–4, 136, 141, 160, 161.
Mahdi, the, 135, 137–8, 141.
Maillet, Monsieur de, 111–14.
Makonnen, Ras, 139, 143, 146, 148, 151, 152, 159–60.
Mangasha, Ras, 137–9, 143.
Massaua, 1, 9, 45–6, 62, 78, 82–3, 85, 88, 90, 92, 95, 99, 100, 103, 121, 124, 132, 137–8, 159.

INDEX

Matthew, 62, 81.
Mendez, Patriarch Alphonzo, 96–9, 101.
Menelik I, King, 12 seqq., 41, 69.
Menelik II, King, 131, 136 seqq., 170, 177.
Michael Suhul, Ras, 121–3, 126–7.
Minas, King, 84, 90, 91.
Monasticism, 5, 35, 73–5, 109–10; among the Falashas, 41.
Murad, 112–13, 116.
Mussolini, Benito, 164–5, 180.

Na'od, King, 55, 80.
Napier, Sir Robert, 20, 132–4, 141, 144, 160.
Nile, River, 1–4, 6, 22, 117, 142, 149–50, 153, 164.
Nine Saints, the, 34–5, 38, 53.
Nubia, the Nubians, 2, 5, 7, 24 note, 25, 29, 44, 47, 67, 127.

Ogaden, 140, 151, 173–4, 177.
Omo, River, 2, 95, 104.
Oviedo, Patriarch Andrew de, 88–93.

Paez, Peter, 92–6, 101.
Papacy, relations with Abyssinia, 52–3, 57–8, 61, 78, 86, 88, 94–6, 99.
Plowden, Walter, 129–32, 135.
Poncet, Monsieur, 111–14.
Portugal, relations with Abyssinia, 3, 6, 44, 61–3, 76 seqq., 98.
Prester John, 59 seqq., 78, 101.

Rasselas, 95 note.
Revenues, 64–6, 195–6, 110.
Roule, Monsieur du, 114–15, 117.
Rudolf, Lake, 1, 2, 151.

Sarsa Dengel, King, 91, 93–4, 98.
Semien, 23, 40, 91.
Sennaar, 67, 112, 115–16, 118, 121, 127.
Shangul, Beni, 130, 151, 157.
Sheba, Queen of, 10 seqq., 17 seqq., 80, 128.

Shoa, 8, 9, 46, 66, 80, 83, 91, 104, 123, 128, 130–1, 136–9, 141, 143, 157, 159, 161, 173.
Sidamo, 161–2, 173.
Sisinnius, King, 94–8, 104, 109.
Slavery, 156, 163, 170–1.
Solomon, 10 seqq., 17 seqq., 41, 80, 116; Solomonian line, 18 seqq., 49, 53–4, 83, 117–18, 120, 126, 138, 158.
Somalis, the, Somaliland, 1, 2, 3, 6–10, 48, 56, 85, 124, 151, 163–4, 173–4.
  British, 141, 148–9, 151, 172, 175, 177.
  French, 141, 146, 176.
  Italian, 137, 140, 151, 153, 176, 177.
Spain, relations with Abyssinia, 94–5.
Suakim, 1, 66, 78, 92, 99, 100.
Sudan, 4, 25, 135, 137, 149, 164, 166, 172.

Tafari, Ras (King Haile Selassie), 159 seqq.
Taitu, Empress, 154–5, 157.
Takazzé, River, 2, 23, 25, 121.
Takla Haymanot, saint, 54, 109–10.
Takla Haymanot I, King, 115, 117.
Takla Haymanot II, King, 123.
Tellez, Balthazar, 101–7.
Tesamma, Ras, 153, 155, 157.
Theodore, King, 128–34, 136, 156.
Theophilus, King, 117.
Tigré, 7, 9, 23, 46, 64–6, 80, 93, 117, 121, 124, 126–31, 134, 137, 139, 143–4, 155, 157, 162, 167–8, 172–3.
Tripartite Treaty, the, 152–3, 164, 179.
Tsana, Lake, 2, 4, 9, 31, 40, 67, 83–5, 95, 105, 108, 128, 131, 149, 153, 163–4, 166, 172.
Turks, the Ottoman, 81–5, 88, 90–2, 95, 101, 103, 124, 150, 158.

Ucciali, Treaty of, 139–40, 142–3, 145.

Walwal, 176–80.
Waragna, 119–20, 122.
Webbe Shibeli, River, 2.
Woldo Giorgis, Ras, 159.
Wollo, the, 9, 123, 136.

Yekuno Amlak, King, 72.

Yemen, 7, 24, 30, 41–2, 46, 83–4, 92.
Za Dengel, King, 93–4.
Zagué dynasty, the, 3, 19–20, 48–9, 52–4.
Zar'a Yakob, King, 55–8, 80.
Zauditu, Empress, 155, 159–62, 167, 170.
Zeila, 46, 48, 78.
Zoscales, King, 22.

PRINTED IN GREAT BRITAIN AT THE UNIVERSITY PRESS, OXFORD
BY JOHN JOHNSON, PRINTER TO THE UNIVERSITY